MW00824545

A Practical Guide to Understanding Ketamine
Treatment & Your Inner Healing Journey

THE
KETAMINE
EFFECT

By: **Dr. Les Cole** (D.Min., CCTP, LPC, CPCS, NBCC)
Dr. Timothy J. Giannoni (Ed.D., MBA, MS)

COPYRIGHT © 2023 LES COLE AND TIMOTHY GIANNONI

All rights reserved.

THE KETAMINE EFFECT

A Practical Guide to Understanding Ketamine Treatment & Your Inner Healing Journey

ISBN   979-8-218-96459-7 *Paperback*

979-8-218-96458-0 *Ebook*

This book is a practical guide to help you understand the potential for change and inner healing through Ketamine Treatment and make informed decisions about your own treatment process. This book is not an academic review of Ketamine's medicinal activation and potential. Instead, we invite you to explore what Ketamine healing can mean for you. Open your mind to new ways of thinking, feeling, and behaving, and talk to your support team about a path toward a deepened relationship with yourself.

CONTENTS

Introduction vii

PART I. THE ROAD TO KETAMINE TREATMENT 1

CHAPTER 1: Our Common & Shared Path Toward Mental Wellness; Understanding the Potential for Ketamine Healing 3
- The Ketamine Effect Key Terms 4
- Our Common Shared Path 6
- The Natural Threat Response 7
- Our Brain and Trauma 10
- The Default Mode Network 11
- The Space Between Self and Others 13
- The Exploration of Transformational Level Change 14
- Three Types of Personal Change 15

CHAPTER 2: Potential Areas of Change & Growth Through the Ketamine Treatment Experience 21
- Ketamine Treatment Overview 22
- Common Ketamine Progression Narrative (C-KPN) Overview 23
- The C-KPN Framework and Interpersonal Change 26
- C-KPN Nine Phases of Ego Development 27
- Ketamine Treatment Phases 30
- The Reality of Change 36

CHAPTER 3: The Path Forward; Actualizing & Exploring the Potential for Change 37

- Learned Helplessness 38
- Enneagram Personality 40
- Waking Up 43
- Actualizing Change as a Result of Ketamine Treatment 45

PART II. WELCOME TO KETAMINE TREATMENT 47

CHAPTER 4: Steps Involved in Ketamine Treatment (Preparation & Support) 49

- Ketamine Assisted Support (KAS) 50
- Common Treatment Protocols 52
- Common Ketamine Progression Narrative (C-KPN) 58
- Areas for Potential Change 59
- Client Reflections 60
- Ketamine Treatment Options 62

CHAPTER 5: Understanding the Healing Perspective, Mechanism of Action: Ketamine Medicine Effect 65

- Ketamine's History 66
- Ketamine's Interaction with Your Brain 66
- Ketamine's Interaction with Your Body 67
- Ketamine's Potential Side Effects 67
- Ketamine Treatment Contraindications 68
- Ketamine Addiction 68
- Routes of Administration 69
- The Ketamine Treatment Environment and Experience 70
- Your Current Medications for Anxiety and/or Depression 72

CHAPTER 6: Making Your Ketamine Treatment Decision 75

- Concern #1: Psychedelic Experience 76
  - » What Does the Psychedelic Effect Entail? 76
  - » Should I be Scared? 78
- Concern #2: Unhealthy Coping Strategies and Ketamine Treatment Readiness 78
  - » How Does Unhealthy Coping Relate to Ketamine Treatment? 79
- Concern #3: Emotional Processing Related to a New Path of Treatment 80
  - » Moving Forward 82

CHAPTER 7: Using C-KPN Conceptual for Self-Directed Work (REFLECTION GUIDES) 85

Ketamine Session Reflection Guides 88

Acknowledgments 128

About the Authors 130

References 132

INTRODUCTION

Are you surviving through life instead of truly living?

The path is long and challenging for most individuals seeking psychiatric or therapeutic support. The questions can be complicated: "How will I ever get better? Is this who I am? Who am I without this part of me?" Because of these thoughts, putting in "the work" through conventional medication or therapy may sometimes feel like an endless journey. Many forms of therapy, medications, and self-help approaches can contribute to temporarily feeling better and lessening symptoms but fail to address and heal the deepest wounds.

If this resonates with you, it means your survival frame of mind, called your Rigid Ego, is in control. Your Rigid Ego is the mind that develops when your unconscious fear of being caught off guard overcomes your inclination for change. Because you "can't" change, your Rigid Ego makes you struggle with despair, excessive worry, hopelessness, and feeling stuck. Your Rigid Ego tells you that your outer world is the cause of distress, and it attaches you to the belief that *if only the outside world would change*, you could find a greater sense of peace.

Unfortunately for your Rigid Ego, the outside world doesn't operate that way. However, you have another Ego inside you begging to come out and help you; this Ego's name is the Fluid Ego.

Your Fluid Ego is a dynamic, robust, and multi-faceted resource that will free your true self, and it's waiting to be explored. No matter how deeply you've traveled inside the Rigid Ego, your Fluid Ego is waiting and has been there all along.

The Rigid Ego is not something bad to get rid of. Rather, it is a part of your whole Ego's ability to be a fluid, robust, and flexible resource. Your survival strategies from the Rigid Ego will always be there for you; they are a genuine part of who you are and protected you at some point. You needed them! They are how you made it to reading this book! But the problem with the Rigid Ego is that it is only a small part of who you most deeply are, yet it parades your life as if it is the whole. It overshadows your awareness and alienates you from your deepest self. Your Rigid Ego keeps you in automatic survival mode reactions, whereas your Fluid Ego observes, assesses, and guides your option to respond, not react. Your Fluid Ego naturally feels "safe" and capable in everyday life. It knows the survival instincts of the Rigid Ego are feelings rather than factual representations of reality.

If you need help breaking through, Ketamine Treatment can be your answer. This book—created with the support of the Attento Ketamine Treatment Team and the contribution of many researchers in this field—will share findings with you about Ketamine Treatment's effects on the Rigid Ego. We've spent more than 1,000 hours directly supporting and working to observe how Ketamine Treatment facilitates the potential for change. With the use of Ketamine medication, the help of a medical support team, and personal healing proactivity, the door is open for your deeper personal exploration.

We will teach you what Ketamine is and how it works in the mind, body, and spirit. You'll learn how Ketamine Treatment may be a healing source if you struggle with treatment-resistant depression, anxiety, or complex trauma. We encourage you to see that there is hope, even if conventional treatments for symptom relief and growth haven't worked for you yet.

MY RIGID EGO STORY

I've observed in myself and others how challenging it is to be stuck in the confines of the Rigid Ego. After 72 years on this planet, including 50 years of practicing psychotherapy, I learned to abandon my Rigid Ego beliefs and see the other side.

My Rigid Ego was built by a complex mixture of family instability in my childhood and the exposure to the unthinkable brutality of war as a young adult enlisted in the United States Armed Forces. After those experiences and traumas, I struggled to find meaning and purpose in my adult life; I was cut off from my true self.

For many years, I felt adrift. I put forth immense personal effort into creating a life that made me feel well-liked, safe, and in control. My contrived sense of attachment helped me survive, but it was also my inevitable breaking point. But then, when I reached that point, I decided to dedicate my life to learning and helping others heal to reconnect with the richness and beauty of who they most deeply are. Now, decades later, my search for an anchor has remained so intense that every new insight is like a cool drop of water on my tongue, tasting like hope.

This 50-year journey led me through three degrees, dozens of jobs, and countless hours spent reflecting on how to be fully human and alive. After a lifetime of confronting the challenges of debilitating panic attacks, pervasive anxiety, and depression, as well as providing psychotherapy to clients grappling with treatment-resistant depression, anxiety, and post-traumatic stress disorder (PTSD), I discovered Ketamine. From practicing as a pastor to a therapist, the most insightful and immediate experiences I have witnessed are the personal transformations from Ketamine Treatment.

In the treatment process, I've seen that individuals can become aware of and challenge the control of the Rigid Ego to break outside that stuckness they're suffering from. Through this Ketamine-assisted level of change, individuals change how they think, feel, and respond by reconnecting with a stronger side of themselves. The reconnection to their inner self reduces depression or anxiety on a medicinal and deeply intrapersonal level. They can have an authentic experience of individuality, personal resilience, and unlock the fullness of themselves—the person who is ready, willing, and not afraid of the change that comes with life's inevitable ebbs and flows. It is truly wonderful to witness.

If you are reading this right now, you've already conquered step one of expanding your Rigid Ego. You are here because change is already unfolding. You are resilient. You are on your way to a better life–a more free and brave way of living!

To All the Mighty Pilgrims Who Wander to and Fro,
Let This Book Be Your Guide Back to Wisdom You Already Know.
All You Ever Really Need Resides Deep Within.
So, To the Brave Who Dare to Look Inward, Your Journey Now Begins.
–DEBI COLE (MY WIFE, LIFE PARTNER & WITNESS TO MY JOURNEY)

PART I

The Road to Ketamine Treatment

1

Our Common & Shared Path Toward Mental Wellness; Understanding the Potential of Ketamine Healing

On behalf of the Attento Ketamine Practice Team, we would like to formally welcome you to this book! We encourage you to have an open mind about your self-reflective journey and the academic content of these chapters as we explore the healing potential of Ketamine Treatment.

Please reflect on the following as we begin:
Ketamine Treatment is a tool for exploring healing.
It is not the source of healing.

Know that there is personal work beyond the medication required in this journey, so we'll introduce chapters to inform and guide you from a personal awareness and a healing perspective. Each chapter will be a journey of expanded awareness, deeper understanding, and self-reflection about Ketamine Treatment—or, for that matter, any form of wellness intervention that supports growth, healing, and a return to your best version of self. We'll provide you with an expansive understanding of the complex interrelationship between your unique individuality–your beliefs, values, identity, experiences, and needs—and the nature of Ketamine Treatment. After reading this, we hope you have a deeper appreciation for personal healing, regardless if Ketamine Treatment is part of your path.

Ketamine Treatment is a single or series of experiences, not a long-term daily medication or weekly therapeutic support session. The Ketamine medication brings you deeper into interpersonal work and understanding of your own potential and readiness to explore many levels of change. In this first chapter, we'll begin with an overview to expand your understanding of the treatment focus and potential areas of impact. Eventually, you'll be able to answer the question:

Is this treatment path right for me?

THE KETAMINE EFFECT KEY TERMS

These definitions are your introduction, so there is no need to worry if they don't stick at first. We'll go more into depth later about what they mean and how they relate to Ketamine Treatment. These concepts will help you understand traditional therapeutic approaches versus enhanced therapeutic work through Ketamine Treatment.

TRAUMA: Confrontation with an event or experience that overwhelms the psychological, physiological, and developmental resources and triggers neurological changes. The neurological changes prime oneself for a life of reacting for survival.[1]

PROTECTIVE EGO FUNCTION: Individualized coping strategy emerging from trauma. The coping strategy redefines "normal" in understanding the self and the world.

RIGID EGO/EGO RIGIDITY: A byproduct of Protective Ego Function. Ego Rigidity resists change and promotes unhealthy thinking patterns, emotional or behavioral reactivity, and survival.[2]

DEFAULT MODE NETWORK: A network of interconnecting brain regions active when one is not focused on what is happening around them. The story of identity, life, and living.[3]

KETAMINE EFFECT: The unique effect of Ketamine medication. Reduces symptoms of anxiety and depression and fosters access to deep resources, resulting in physiological and psychological change.

COMMON KETAMINE PROGRESSION NARRATIVE (C-KPN): Pronounced See-Cap-En. A framework for understanding potential physiological and psychological transformation through Ketamine Treatment.

KETAMINE ASSISTED SUPPORT (KAS): Counseling/coaching support guiding the exploration of physiological and psychological change.

TRANSFORMATIONAL CHANGE: A deeper level of change. A new perspective of personal functioning where an individual is actively searching for solutions. Each path is different depending on the uniqueness driven by choice.[4]

AUTHENTIC/ESSENTIAL SELF: A stronger sense of self that is more complex, robust, and adaptable in the ability to broadly experience reality without distortions; lends itself to deeper understanding and responding to daily life with authenticity.

OUR COMMON SHARED PATH

To begin our journey, let's first reflect and embrace what we call "our common shared path." This is the idea that *everyone* shares the experience of moving through struggle and actively searching for solutions— even though each path differs depending on individuality and current phase in life. Life is challenging and entails weathering many storms. We all seek the strength to weather those storms, and the test of our strength becomes evident when we move through knowing that we are adaptable and strong. We all navigate trauma; you are not alone in what you are facing!

A single significant life event or the weakening by a thousand cuts defines a common path for all humans and highlights how trauma shapes who we are. In many respects, to be alive involves exposure to trauma. Historically, the definition of trauma has been limited to life and death scenarios (e.g., combat, car wrecks, observed or experienced acts of violence, etc.); however, this limited focus misses all of the developmental traumas we experience as we grow and develop. Anyone who has suffered the loss of a loved one, a pet, a job, a divorce, or been confronted with the potential of a devastating illness knows trauma! Anyone who has spent horrifying moments in the dark at 2:30 a.m. when the full awareness of our own, or those we love, mortality knows trauma! Anyone marginalized, bullied, or devalued in their formative years knows trauma!

As we grow, experience, and process trauma, we each develop a Protective Ego Function to keep us safe and guide our life journey. The loss of safety, referred to as triggers, is felt as anxiety or depression. These feelings signal automatic, sometimes unconscious, reactions from the impact of past trauma.

As we grow and our experiences become more diverse, so does our Protective Ego Function. Each of us has a personality that's a byproduct of our desire to live with a level of certainty about who we are, what we believe, and what keeps us safe in our relationships with others and the world. Our experience with trauma, uncertainties, or changes may make us feel unprotected and as though we do not have a healthy perspective to guide our own adaptability.

THE NATURAL THREAT RESPONSE

Understanding the effects of emotional pain in your life requires you to recognize that trauma, in all its forms, triggers a predatory and prey response. Like a deer crossing a street and freezing at the sight of a car, any time something comes along and catches you off guard, your predatory detection system kicks in to try to protect you. When your brain perceives a threat, your sympathetic nervous system (automatic and often unconscious reactive tendency) is activated and initiates a fight, flight, freeze, or fawn response. Let's review examples of how these responses may play out in your life.

Type of Reaction	Definition	Example
Fight	A fight reaction is when a person feels a need or obligation to react aggressively through voice or behavior; the intensity of the response does not match the vulnerability of the situation.	Taylor drives to the grocery store to pick up ingredients for dinner. As Taylor pulls into a parking spot, someone yells, "Nice driving, jerk!" Taylor's threat response is activated, and Taylor fires back by giving the middle finger and cursing.
Flight	A flight reaction is a self-protective reaction of moving away and not addressing the situation (also known as avoidance).	Parker avoids commitment at all costs. He receives a text from a friend asking for support with a moving project. The request for commitment activates his threat response. Parker does not respond to the text until after the moving date. He responds by telling his friend that he never saw the text.

Freeze	A freeze reaction is when an option for response is not accessible; the individual becomes trapped in not responding.	Avery has a dentist appointment today at 9 a.m., but she has hated the dentist since having a painful root canal a few years ago. Avery's threat response is activated. As time passes, Avery stares at the clock, unable to move. Before she realizes it, 9 a.m. has passed, and Avery has stayed home, missing the appointment.
Fawn	A fawn reaction is when an individual makes a conscious effort to defuse a situation while not addressing the area of concern (also known as people pleasing).	Morgan just started dating a new partner, and they have not argued yet. However, today his partner seems to be in a bad mood. Morgan worries that conflict may arise because of their bad mood, so his threat response is activated.
		He fawns by doing everything he can to make his partner happy. He cleans his partner's house, buys them dinner, and shows more affection than normal. Even when his partner is upsetting Morgan, he does anything to keep the peace, most frequently by suspending his awareness and expression of his own wants, needs, thoughts, and feelings.

Think of the last time you felt afraid and acted in a fight, flight, freeze, or fawn response:

- Can you relate to Taylor, Parker, Avery, or Morgan and their immediate reaction tendencies?
- Think about situations in your day-to-day life. Can you relate to the quick transition between your calm state and the fight/flight/freeze/fawn reaction?
- Do you know your triggers? Are they frequently being experienced?
- Do you sometimes feel like you "blacked out" or that something took over you in these states?
- Do you ever feel exhausted as a result of these tendencies?

There is a physiological component to these reaction tendencies. Cortisol, a hormone that increases blood sugar and suppresses the immune system to redirect our energy onto the perceived threat, is released during the fight, flight, freeze, and fawn response. This fear response starts in a region of the brain called the amygdala—an almond-shaped structure in the brain's temporal lobe that detects the emotional importance of the experience (stimuli).[5] Recent research suggests that information about potentially threatening experiences reaches the amygdala before we even know that there is something to be afraid of.[6]

The thalamus to amygdala pathway that runs from the reaction centers of the brain is similar to a superhighway. This superhighway registers the sensory information as a threat needing to be feared before our thinking center (cerebral cortex) knows anything is happening. The threat response is an uncontrollable reaction from your body's brain-based processing system (threat detection system). This tendency has been learned and made "normal" through the years, only becoming a habit as we react in patterned ways.

OUR BRAIN AND TRAUMA

Trauma can actually result in mind-level change that traps us in reactive patterns. It can severely affect how we think, feel, and behave, even as adults.[7] When we're in survival mode for too long, we become hypervigilant and constantly scan for threats to prevent getting caught off guard. Although the reaction readiness of our body and mind is protective, it may result in our cerebral cortex (*the rational thinking portion of the brain that interprets events or experiences to decide response options*) losing its processing ability. More simply stated, traumatic events may hardwire our brains to react to the "next" perceived threat, even if a threat is not present. Instead of generating a response to a threat through exploring, pondering, or mental modeling, our brain's fight, flight, freeze, or fawn reaction kicks in automatically.[8] Although our brain thinks it's protecting us, the over-functioning of this scanning system can deteriorate into a system of false alarms (perceptual distortions) triggered by the Protective Ego Function. From here, letting our guard down will trigger a threat response, which makes us resist change.

Imagine a sheep grazing in a field and hearing a loud noise. The sheep's automatic reaction is to run away from the sound and keep running until it feels like the threat is gone. Once it knows the potential threat is out of reach, it relaxes and returns to grazing. Now, imagine if the sheep never stopped running! For many of us, the experiences of our own life can create this heightened state of reaction versus having fuller access to our many response options. We may find ourselves constantly triggered or feeling ever-present anxiety or depression, but we may actually be overreacting.

The feeling of constant threat is mentally, physically, and spiritually exhausting. Anxiety and depression become traveling companions, holding onto worry and hopelessness toward life. These companions pull us further and further from the best version of ourselves, promising that it is all in the name of self-protection.

We know it may seem impossible, but challenging your sense of self helps you discover newness in relationships and experiences; it enables you to move past your unhealthy "normal." This movement expands your awareness and fuels your capacity to explore meaningful change.

THE DEFAULT MODE NETWORK

Individuality is the extension of your body-mind unconscious knowing and your brain's conscious awareness. Together and unique to you as an individual, these influences shape the perceptions of the life you've lived and are ever evolving through. This system, known as the Default Mode Network (DMN), guides your day-to-day life and establishes your "normal."

The DMN can be best understood as your internal active voice—the one you "talk to" when you are passively thinking. This voice reflects the story of who you are and the world around you; it is the ever-present narrative in your head.[11] It is your created story that functions across time to make life and your identity dependable and constant. Because you have your own story and perspectives, your life experiences are a filtered reality.

Your DMN is mostly active when you're not focused on the outside world and your brain is at wakeful rest, such as during mind-wandering.[12] It is also active when thinking about others, thinking about yourself, remembering the past, and planning for the future. Though the concept may seem foreign at first, it is something we all experience daily. We can all relate to the experience of taking a familiar route to work, "zoning out", arriving, and wondering how we made it without having paid attention. Other examples are our quiet internal reflections, final thoughts right before falling asleep, daydreams, or our mind during a creative task. In these moments, our thoughts continue to fill the space without external stimuli that require our attention.

Does your DMN reflect peace within yourself through positive messaging or involve a negative spiral of unhealthy worry?

Self-reflect on where your mind goes when you experience a DMN moment. Is it worrying about an event from yesterday? Is it ruminating on an embarrassing moment from 30 years ago? Is it thinking of being lesser than others? Is it a hopeful daydream about the future? DMN activity constructs a belief about "how life is" in your mind. An unhealthy DMN can continually hijack the mind to message a negative view of self or circumstance.

Some examples of unhealthy DMN overactivity include:

- Being stuck in a loop of negative thinking about the past; remembering failure, challenges, or being devalued.
- Preoccupation with past traumatic experiences occupying present thoughts; feeling vulnerable or in danger.
- Not being able to relax; feeling constant anxiety or depression even when in a restful state.
- Experiencing racing thoughts with yourself as the central reference point; harboring a negative perspective of others or events.
- Not being present for experiences; seeking distraction and separation to withdraw from the moment's reality.

DMN messaging known only to you is a powerful force influencing daily perception. The DMN actively shapes your interpretation of experience and often limits your ability to respond proactively versus react. For instance, if you constantly think about embarrassing moments of the past, the narrative spinning in your mind is that you are an embarrassing person. This narrative makes you always feel on edge while trying to avoid embarrassing yourself again. Awareness of DMN's functioning is essential to your readiness for transformation change. Still, no matter how your DMN functions now, it can change. Your narrative can change!

THE SPACE BETWEEN SELF AND OTHERS

D. W. Winnicott, trauma-informed psychotherapy, and the Polyvagal theory identify the area of personal growth and development as the space between self and others, not what is wrong within us.[9] You have the opportunity to change when expanding your awareness and understanding of how your relationships and experiences have shaped you. A change in a personal perspective guides you on a path toward mental wellness, growth, and healing.

Human beings are flexible. We are not born with a roadmap for personality and Ego development. Yes, we all start with parts of our individuality—DNA influences, physical attributes, temperament—but the interaction of these features with the world around us develops our unique self. Development unfolds in the space between ourselves and others.

We can look to Erickson's stage theory of development to further dive into this concept. This theory identifies our first stage of human development as the passive stage. In the passive stage, from birth to 12 months, Erickson's theory states that we only view awareness between "self and other" with the perspective of trust or mistrust (for example: a baby crying when held by anyone but their parent).

The next stage, which occurs from 18-36 months, involves the development of a distinction between "self and other."[10] This developmental milestone is frequently announced by our first use of the word "no." The power of "no" is followed by a greater awareness of self and seeing that the self/psyche/Ego is a distinct reality apart from others (expression of personal autonomy and independence). From this point, our developmental path involves reacting and responding to relationships with others and the world. We are radically open beings in immediate and intimate contact with one another. We aren't meant to be closed-off or independent entities expected to figure out others from a distance.

The healing process begins with recognizing that symptoms such as depression or anxiety are not conflicts between internal drives and external demands—dysregulation caused by external triggers. Instead, these symptoms are evidence that something has happened to us, whether that be trauma or some other deficit in our relationships (e.g., instability, unpredictability of family of origin, abuse, neglect, insecure attachment, encounter with significant adverse life events, etc.). These developmental influences create a predetermined lens from which we view the world. We often think of our center as "in our head," but we actually have a body-mind experience. Our mind is embedded in our body, holding onto traumatic lessons from our lives. Understanding these influences on the mind sparks the question:

With all the influences that have made us who we are, can we change and nurture a healthier mind?

THE EXPLORATION OF TRANSFORMATIONAL LEVEL CHANGE

As expressed in Winnicottian theory focusing on developmental influences, human relationships can both hurt and heal psychological change.[13] Therapy, and Ketamine Treatment specifically, is a co-creative journey in the transitional space between you and your wellness support professional. In the transitional space, you and a support person (therapist/coach) connect in a private space void of judgment or expectation. In this connection, the support person offers an exploratory environment for present and historical aspects of life experiences that are too painful or overwhelming to dive into without guidance and support. In and from this space, you and the support person move down the path toward greater levels of personal awareness to unearth a new perspective of your healthier version of self: transformational level change.

During Ketamine Treatment, you realize how the Rigid Ego controls your perspective and limits your ability to consider and actualize change. Let's review the three types of change according to Mary Blast and Clarence Thomson.[4]

THREE TYPES OF PERSONAL CHANGE

Type of Change:	Definition:	Examples:
First Order Change	Behavioral change: learning a new skill or capability. It doesn't require any loss or change in your beliefs or view of yourself and the world. It only requires information you did not know prior. The Ego learns and enriches.	Alex suffers from frequent panic attacks. His mental health care guide recommends that he practice the 5-4-3-2-1 coping technique for anxiety: count backward slowly and with each number, breathe, and invite slowing down to relax. Alex's panic attacks don't go away, but he learns to calm himself down sometimes.
Second Order Change	Change from the perspective of self to another. Illusions about how the world functions or exists are eliminated. New possibilities emerge and a new perspective fundamentally changes you. The Ego morphs and believes it is different.	Sally is terrified of public speaking and immediately begins to sweat and shut down if she has to talk in a group. Using personal affirmations, Sally reminds herself she is a "great public speaker" to reaffirm her belief that she is capable. She finds a willingness to share her voice and becomes more confident in her ability to publicly speak as she begins to believe in herself.

| Transformational Change | Point of view shifts as the center of executive functioning moves from the restrictive domain of the Rigid Ego to the observing self.

The observing self recognizes the Rigid Ego's influences and uses those as only a part of the decision-making process. This shift opens the perceptual frameworks, facilitating a less distorted view of reality.

You're empowered to initiate continual change spontaneously and create your experience of life moment-to-moment. You distinguish yourself as the **changer** and not that which is being changed. | With a challenging upbringing filled with trauma, Jesse questions her self-worth and personal value to others. Avoidance and being unnoticed protect her from these feelings.

Supported in her journey, Jesse re-writes her life story to be one of resilience and surviving her past difficulties. She recognizes her trauma is something that happened to her, not who she is. Her new perspective provides her options to explore experiences and relationships looking forward. |

Ketamine Treatment is focused on transformational change level work. The medication is used as a tool to reduce anxiety and depression and dissociate from your familiar Ego. The dissociation from your "normal" Ego frees you to consider substantive changes. Freedom unlocks a different perspective for understanding yourself and the trauma you've experienced.

Your change readiness challenge involves you exploring your day-to-day Ego orientation and DMN state and reflecting on how this has developed and became your "normal." When you challenge yourself this way, you can access the unlimited potential of continuous change for healthier interpersonal balance. Consider this as an important question in your Ketamine Treatment decision:

Am I seeking transformational level change?
What would those changes look like?

Ketamine acts as an agent to reduce symptoms of anxiety and depression, thus providing greater access to inner healing through understanding that change is possible. Beyond the confines of Ego Rigidity and the automatic function of the DMN, it is possible to reset the mind-body system and find a space to explore change. Transformational level change in Ketamine Treatment goes beyond acquiring a new coping skill (1st Order Change), beyond a change of view or perspective of ourselves (2nd Order Change), and to an awareness of our observing self with the full capacity to be the agent of change (3rd Order Change).[14]

We will examine the many sides of Ketamine in the remainder of the book, but for now, view the Ketamine Effect using the framing of our Common Ketamine Progression Narrative (C-KPN) model:

Reduction of Symptoms of Anxiety/Depression

↓

Mind Level Exploration of Ego-Level Awareness and Potential for Change

↓

Exploration of Transformational Level Change (Reconnection to Essential Self & Improved Capacity to Respond and Not React)

↓

Reconnection to Healthier Life and Living

As a person seeking a return to a better version of self, we encourage you to find a compassionate medical support team, therapist, or specialist to accompany you on the road back to you. We invite you to engage with professionals who understand that therapeutic work involves the deeper exploration of Ego functioning and acknowledge that intrapersonal trauma is relevant to the healing process. The depth of this level of therapeutic work goes beyond anxiety and depressive symptom management. This journey requires vulnerability, openness to explore, awareness of personal resilience, and acknowledging the impact of your trauma.

Ketamine Treatment can facilitate the release of the restrictive control of the Protective Ego Function for the emergence and awareness of the expanded Ego capacity for transformational change. The combination of Ketamine and Ketamine Assisted Support (KAS) fosters a potential return to the more of you than the protective and controlling Rigid Ego will easily allow.

Welcome to the perspective of deeper personal reflection and awareness that Ketamine Treatment can offer through inner healing work. Welcome to the journey back to you.

REMEMBER...

- Change is an "inside job" best accomplished with support.
- Trauma is a shared reality of life–common to us all.
- You can't change anyone or anything but yourself.
- Your Ego is flexible and can accommodate change.
- Embrace the Self: Observe! Observe! Observe! Grow through understanding!
- You do not have to know everything; you need only the vulnerability to look inside yourself more deeply.
- The work of exploring change can happen when the weight of anxiety and depression is lightened.

QUESTIONS FOR REFLECTION

- Do you believe the symptoms of anxiety or depression reflect something that "happened" to you vs. something "wrong" with you?
- How would you rate your Ego Rigidity (low/medium/high)?
- Do you genuinely accept that "Ego is an interpersonal reality that can change through exploring unique experiences"?
- Can you identify the active working of your DMN—healthy and unhealthy?
- Are you open to professional support and perspective to guide you in the journey toward change that requires vulnerability?

2

Potential Areas of Change & Growth Through the Ketamine Treatment Experience

CLIENT REFLECTION:
After many Ketamine treatments I became aware of the expansive nature of the experience; it is always different. Focusing on the experience, I have recognized familiar feelings of space and possibilities that continue to be explored. I wrestle with the question of what is changing—I KNOW SOMETHING IS!

Until recently, the generally accepted academic belief was that brain-based connections are established early in life and are highly resistant to change. However, evidence has since emerged demonstrating that that is not the case. It is becoming more broadly accepted that our brains have the capacity for neuroplasticity (creation of new connections) beyond our early years of development.[1]

The key to unlocking neuroplasticity is through brain activation—enter The Ketamine Effect. This exceptional property has captured the attention of the psychiatric community and sparked research into how Ketamine affects the brain's functioning. Ketamine as an intervention for treatment-resistant anxiety or depression through any form of administration (nasal, tablets, intravenous, or intramuscular injection) provided by a qualified medical provider can have profound effects, acting as an agent for improving symptoms and overall functioning.

Ketamine works through neurotransmitters (connections within and between brain regions) that are not activated through typical anxiety or depression medications. It activates the glutamate messaging centers of the brain and excites areas of the brain that become engaged during the Ketamine Treatment experience (details of this activation to be covered in a later chapter). Once activated, brain chemistry can change. The response to Ketamine Treatment and the experience itself is always unique to the individual; however, it's common to experience anxiety and depression symptom reduction for a brief or extended period after treatment.

With that being said, one of the hardest truths about Ketamine Treatment is that change isn't achieved just by doing Ketamine. Change comes from *within*. Research has found that someone's personal commitment to change is more important to treatment success than the method of intervention, the skill of the practitioner, or the relationship with their support person.[2] This is not said to diminish the positive and sometimes needed support of psychiatric medication to lessen symptoms. Still, true interpersonal transformational work begins when you feel prepared, open and ready to experience change.

Ketamine's medicinal effects allow a window of opportunity for you to enter change beyond symptom reduction, unlock hidden parts of your healthy Ego, and hold onto those parts—if you so choose. The effects allow you to connect your experience to your real life for renowned ways of thinking, feeling, and behaving.

KETAMINE TREATMENT OVERVIEW

Before we continue, please be aware there are both Federal Drug Administration (FDA) and best practice Clinical Treatment Guidelines for determining client appropriateness for Ketamine Treatment. Only medically supervised use of sub-sedation Ketamine for the purpose of symptom reduction is advocated for in this book.

The Ketamine Treatment experience is usually 45 to 90 minutes. However, the dissociation experience during Ketamine Treatment has a potential long-term impact on both your brain-based functioning and Ego state. The dissociation experience turns off your fight, flight, freeze, and fawn response, so you can review emotionally charged situations or concepts without a physical reaction to reconnect to a deeper level of mindfulness that you forgot existed. We've consistently found that the dissociative properties create an opportunity for re-association with your Authentic Self that is resilient, adaptable to change, and has the capacity to respond instead of react. Examples of potential areas of change through Ketamine Treatment include:

- Freedom of relief from anxiety and depression
- Re-processing traumatic experiences and seeing them from a new perspective (ex: having a greater capacity for emotional neutrality)
- Reconnecting to the Essential Self that may be forgotten or inaccessible
- Active exploration of DMN tendencies
- Greater recognition of a capacity to respond and not react
- Feeling freedom from the confines of Rigid Ego thinking
- Exploration of unhealthy coping patterns

This window of opportunity is referred to as the integration phase of treatment—the active exploration of your potential to explore change. To help your understanding, let's move to C-KPN and discuss how Ketamine can open the window for change through treatment.

C-KPN OVERVIEW

The Common Ketamine Progression Narrative (C-KPN) identifies areas of personal history and functioning that may be affected by Ketamine Treatment. With our team's years of experience with Ketamine Treatment facilitation, C-KPN is a psychological perspective that offers insight into mind-level change. Beyond the brain-based effect of Ketamine, there are also psychological factors (thinking, emotional, behavioral) that may change from treatment. Identifying what you need to work on in these areas is crucial in determining your benefits. Take a moment here to ask yourself:

How can I change my mental wellness?

Here are some ideas to get your thoughts flowing:

- Increase confidence
- Reset from unhealthy patterns of feeling, thinking, and/or behavior rooted in past traumatic experiences
- Remember life without constant anxiety and/or depression
- Be less reactive and more proactive in recognizing response options
- Embrace self-compassion
- Increase capacity to deal with the ups and downs of life

Whatever the change may be, remember: you don't have to change in every area. Change is hard, and it takes time! As an experience-driven treatment, the potential change effect after treatment may be the most important aspect. Ketamine Treatment and C-KPN can potentially help you find the root of your symptoms and behaviors. By embracing the C-KPN framework as a starting point, you and your professional support team can have meaningful conversations about desired change and improvement.

C-KPN requires the diagnosis of treatment-resistant depression, anxiety, or PTSD during your Ketamine Treatment intake process. This diagnosis acknowledges that Ketamine Treatment is appropriate for you. After determining your appropriateness for Ketamine Treatment, C-KPN guides the treatment change potential. The following table provides an overview of potential change areas through Ketamine Treatment (not presented in order of priority):

Potential Area of Psychological Change	C-KPN Progression: What potentially could change as a result of Ketamine Treatment
General State of Functioning (Medical Treatment Benefit)	Potential to improve baseline anxiety, depression, social engagement, and general lifestyle functioning. SIMPLE SUMMARY: Decreased symptoms of anxiety or depression that improve overall functioning.
Ego Rigidity (Psychological Treatment Benefit)	Expand Ego awareness away from automatic self-protective response tendencies. Experience a greater feeling of understanding and potential control of the DMN. An exploration of mind-level change for healthier options. SIMPLE SUMMARY: Potential for greater wellness through Ego awareness. Reaching Ego Fluidity.
Adverse Childhood Experience (ACE) and/or Significant Life Traumatic Event(s) Impacting Lifestyle Functioning (PTSD/ Trauma Response) (Psychological Treatment Benefit)	Ability to revisit, examine, and process past adverse or traumatic experiences with greater emotional neutrality. Transitioning from the negative emotional memory of said events to finding greater emotional balance in present functioning. SIMPLE SUMMARY: Potential to emotionally unwind.
Personality Re-Orientation (Psychological Treatment Benefit)	Reconnecting to Essential Self through understanding personality tendencies. Opportunity to ponder the adaptability. SIMPLE SUMMARY: Recognition, awareness, and acceptance of Authentic/Essential Self.

Self-Medication (Psychological Treatment Benefit)	Ketamine medicine creates a possible positive impact on both physiological and emotional dependence to self-medication and unhealthy coping. Progression means moving toward healing with healthier coping strategies for lessened emotional pain. SIMPLE SUMMARY: Potential to explore healthier coping.

Personal progress with the support of your mental wellness team can help focus you on changing in one, several, or all of the areas above. Take a moment to reflect on these areas and ask yourself:

If I could go beyond the lessening of symptoms of anxiety and depression, what do I need or want in terms of deeper healing and mind-level change?

THE C-KPN FRAMEWORK AND INTERPERSONAL CHANGE

After sitting back and contemplating these five areas of C-KPN potential change, you might be thinking, "Aren't these the same psychological areas of potential change that are the focus of psychiatric medication, healing support, or general positive wellness practice?" The answer to this question is indeed yes. The value of therapeutic and psychiatric support is *not* replaced by Ketamine Treatment. Rather, Ketamine Treatment allows you to focus more *intensely* on these areas. Ketamine Treatment has a more immediate effect on your symptoms, so it's possible to travel further inward for personal healing. Unlike psychiatric medicine, therapy, or wellness endeavors focusing on *lessening* symptoms, Ketamine gives you a faster and deeper level of interpersonal experience focusing on doing "real-time" transformational-level work that goes even further.

Ketamine Treatment doesn't focus on what might be "wrong with you" (pathology—something is broken). Instead, it focuses on how your Ego Rigidity and the Default Mode Network (DMN) cause you to have limited readiness or willingness to explore change. It then takes this information and uses your awareness of your Ego's tendencies and manifestations—like coping mechanisms—to entice transformational change. This work changes you from within, without relying on your life situation to change (however, it is *POSSIBLE* that this level of change can affect your life circumstances).

This change from within means the discovery of inner resources previously blocked by the Rigid Ego and willingness to have *reasonable* expectations for your potential for change. A client reflection post Ketamine session highlights this potential change and expanded personal awareness:

> *"My capacity for greater personal accountability to the needs of others plus my commitments equals me feeling happy with myself."*

You aren't reinventing yourself. Instead, you are exploring the capacity for change that may result in you having greater access to a better, more authentic version of self. Talking with your mental health care team about what is reasonable versus unreasonable can help guide you.

Often defined by moments of clarity or connection, Ketamine Treatment offers a glimpse into the active working of the Rigid Ego, DMN, and the repressed, forgotten aspects of your dynamic, robust, and Essential Self. The treatment experience can confirm your potential for change and growth and show you that you have the power to evolve. You may experience movement and the freedom of being present and empowered by knowing that you have the choice to heal. A contemplation of this kind of intrapersonal and interpersonal change only comes from within.

C-KPN NINE PHASES OF EGO DEVELOPMENT

The following chart contains the C-KPN nine phases of Ego development and the Ego stage and phase level experience that goes along with characteristics for each level. Although there is no good or bad starting point of Ego level functioning, the awareness of your current level of Ego functioning provides a deeper understanding of your future path for potential change. Transformation potential exists if you aspire to it! It's not easy, but Ketamine can be a unique tool in your transformation.

C-KPN EGO LEVELS, EGO STAGE & PHASES OF KETAMINE EXPERIENCE

C-KPN Ego Levels of Development (Orientation of how you feel and experience life)	C-KPN Ego Stage (Ego awareness & path for transformation)	Ketamine Phase Level Experience (Time spent in experience, what might be expected)
RESTRICTED STAGE:		
Level 1: • Absolute Ego Rigidity • Loss of Openness; Separated from Life	Survival Ego Stage; Constant sense of threat & emotional imbalance	**Phase 1:** Unwinding/ Re-Processing
Level 2: • Dependence on Thinking and Emotional Perception to Validate Sense of Threat	Survival Ego Stage; Belief that change may not be possible	**Phase 1:** Unwinding/ Re-Processing
Level 3: • Emerging Awareness of Threat Leads to Seeking Control of Self and/or Others	Survival Ego Stage; Focus is on external instead of internal change	**Phase 1:** Unwinding/ Re-Processing

EMERGING STAGE:		
Level 4: • Awareness of Emerging Emotional Damage Due to Attempts to Control Self & Others	Emerging tensions between openness and Rigid Ego Stage; Expanded personal awareness & connection	**Phase 2:** Mindful/Aware/ Active: Contemplation and Exploration of Meaningful Interpersonal Change
Level 5: • Openness is Restricted by Prevailing Fear, Shame, Guilt and Need to Control	Emerging tensions between openness and Rigid Ego Stage; Reflections and realizations	**Phase 2:** Mindful/Aware/ Active: Contemplation & Exploration of Meaningful Interpersonal Change
Level 6: • Need to Control Replaced by Openness and Ability to Observe (More Objective/ Honest View of Self, Others & Life Experiences)	Emerging tensions between openness and Rigid Ego Stage; Letting go of need to control	**Phase 2:** Mindful/Aware/ Active: Contemplation & Exploration of Meaningful Interpersonal Change
ACTUALIZING STAGE:		
Level 7: • Open to Seeing Needs of Self and Others. • Access to Choices • No Need or Obligation to React.	Ego flexibility and resilience Stage; healthy unbounded perspective	**Phase 3:** Aspirational/Adaptable: Executive Functioning Shift/ Self as Agent of Change
Level 8: • Feeling Emotions, not Being Defined by Them	Ego flexibility and resilience Stage; exploration of emotional response options	**Phase 3:** Aspirational/Adaptable: Executive Functioning Shift/ Self as Agent of Change
Level 9: • Freedom to Observe • Choosing to Respond or Not	Ego flexibility and resilience Stage; freedom to choose, emotion serves to support decision making	**Phase 3:** Aspirational/Adaptable: Executive Functioning Shift/ Self as Agent of Change

LEVELS 1-3:

Levels 1-3 are the reality for many when they begin Ketamine Treatment. These levels are distant from remembering or seeing the potential on the other side. Often, 1-3 represents someone stuck in the tight grip of anxiety and depression or dealing with the complexity of PTSD/ trauma. The rigidity of the Ego traps them in patterns of feeling hopeless, hypervigilant, and isolated.

LEVELS 4-6:

Levels 4-6 highlight a "need to control" orientation. Individuals in these levels have tension between starting to want to explore change while still having the Ego Rigidity attempting to stay in power.

LEVELS 7-9:

Levels 7-9 are a state of actualization. Individuals in these levels find the freedom of choice to respond versus react and are empowered through their decisions to live life with a healthy Ego balance.

Through honest and personal self- reflection, we challenge you to find your Ego Level on the chart.

KETAMINE TREATMENT PHASES

Through our team's administration of over 1,000 hours of Ketamine Treatment sessions with direct support, we've also created a Phase of Experience chart that is displayed below. This chart captures the experiential parts of the treatment experience and its relation to the transformation of the Ego.

The movement of clients through these phases is not linear. Progression and familiarity with the stages of Ego change over time and the number of Ketamine sessions play a role in each individual's journey. These changes suggest that treatment is supported through continued experiences. Four sessions are generally needed to become familiar with the Ketamine Effect experience and to determine appropriate dosing.

Still, sessions may continue beyond this number as you find the value of Ketamine intervention and the change effects. With movement through the Ketamine Treatment Phases, there are actual observable changes in Ego level fuctioning. Active change is made possible because of changes in our neuroplasticity (how our brain is wired). Through treatment, Ketamine Assisted Support (KAS) helps clients in moving to higher states of Ego awareness and providing greater access to inner healing outside of the treatment experience.

CLIENT PHASE 1 KETAMINE EXPERIENCE-RESTRICTIVE
(Typical of Ego Levels and Stages 1-3):

- Uncertain about the self-healing nature or context nature of experience; questioning experience value and how they might benefit from it

- Feeling closed in small spaces or underwater

- General discomfort with the experience of being still, voids, and darkness; desire/expectation of something different

- Client not understanding entry into experience, having limited depth or early transition from experience; anxiety/uncertainty/need to know if doing it right

- Wrestling with Ego; early exploring with letting go (clients can articulate post-session interaction with the Ego Bubble)

- Feelings of early symptom reduction (anxiety/depression/PTSD/emotional memory) during the experience

- Exploration of characters, experiences, and issues from the past

- Past/current trauma exploration; may feel a sense of "emotional neutrality" during revisiting past experiences

- Desire to control and maintain "normal awareness" during the experience

- Client actively seeking comfort during the experience and checking in through physical movement to stay grounded with conscious self

- Experiencing Ketamine Voice; having a hard time sharing details of Ketamine Treatment experience

- Worried about the time and role of medical professionals providing support

- Client early or abrupt exit from experience; often quiet and reflective

- Client not understanding intention exploration/not being able to reflect on or hold on to intention during the experience

CLIENT PHASE 2 KETAMINE EXPERIENCE-EMERGING
(Typical of Ego Levels and Stages 4-6):

- Signs of being eager for experience; clients arrive prepared, excited, and talkative

- Desire and interest to direct experience; greater ability to define and explore the intention of the experience

- Expressed desire for deeper experience

- Increasing reports of images, colors, or feelings associated with being strong and centered

- Loss of physical body connection during the experience (feeling of being singular); fully letting go of the construct of time

- Transition to spiritual connection (existential exploration, belief in things beyond self, wonder)

- Feeling of immense space and personal freedom to direct and explore

- Realizing change of symptoms (depression/anxiety) during and after the experience

- Feelings of mindfulness and access to a great sense of peace, connection with self and their world

- Somatic (physical) feeling of source energy & connection; enjoyment in the drift

- Exploring unique, sometimes forgotten parts of self; self-kindness and more positive acceptance

- Expanded articulation of parts of self that may require change

- Finding joy in being, feeling free from burden

- Success in moving through the Ego Bubble; brief period of feeling freer and at ease/recognition of something healthier on the other side

- Extended session time; willingness to stay with experience/no need for early exit and not concerned about medical or support team time

CLIENT PHASE 3 KETAMINE EXPERIENCE-ACTUALIZING
(Typical of Ego Levels and Stages 7-9):

• Concrete recognition of personal change and ability to define (less anxious/less depressed)

• Existential preoccupation (feeling positive and hopeful)

• No longer feeling stuck

• Finding it easier to complete tasks, feeling purposeful, feeling a connection to familiar healthier patterns of cognition, spirituality, social connection, and physical wellness

• Recognition of past unhealthy or maladaptive patterns (thinking, relational, behaviors)

• Different relationship with past trauma; access to greater emotional neutrality (movement from event to how it impacted thinking/behavior/emotions)

• Ability to articulate what has changed and how the world and people around them are reflecting back apparent change

• Reduction of hyper-vigilance

• Expanded personal adaptability and balance in life

• Improved self-esteem and efficacy

- Sessions center around using experience to explore greater balance and personal growth

- Client directed intention setting and integration

- Need and willingness to share experience with others, recognizing the importance of experience in personal change

- Discussion about possibilities; fewer familiar feelings of limitation.

- Decrease in episodes of depression/anxiety; pattern change (less intensity/depth—symptoms become transient, and client feels an improved ability to cope and manage)

- Client freely shares the most vulnerable side(s) of self without concern of judgment or shame; the person's true nature is revealed in terms of deepest fears, worries, and concerns of negative self-perception

PHASE 1 reflects the strongest presence and control of the Rigid Ego. The Rigid Ego resists surrendering to the experience of exploration.

PHASE 2 reflects the relaxing of the Rigid Ego and entrance of the observing Ego. The emergence of the observing Ego is shown by a greater ability to go with the flow, emerging openness, and willingness to experience the healing power of being mindful.

PHASE 3 reflects even fuller emergence of the observing Ego. The Fluid Ego takes over the executive function role to observe and explore transformation-level change.

Once your Ego Level/Stage is established, you and your treatment team will be better equipped to support your preparation for your Ketamine experiences and track your progress over time. We encourage you to identify your phase of experience throughout treatment and utilize this framework to see how a change in your level of Ego orientation facilitates inner healing and awareness.

THE REALITY OF CHANGE

Ketamine Treatment is all about creating space for change. Still, change can be challenging, scary, or bring grief from losing something familiar to us. Good or bad, change requires the loss of something that has been. The Ketamine experience can potentially change you, but it's unlike most changes you are familiar with. You may be losing something familiar, but it's something that's tying you down. Like a balloon that must be let go to soar, exploring the fullness of your Ego Fluidity and adaptability requires you to let go of familiar patterns of thinking, emotions, and reactions.

REMEMBER...

- Change doesn't happen without putting in the work.
- Change is scary and challenging—but worth it.
- Ketamine can open your mind to new perspectives about your past, present, and future.
- There are three types of change: First Order, Second Order, and Transformational.
- There are three stages of our Ego: restricted, emerging, and actualizing.
- No matter where we are with our Ego, we can let go and expand.
- Change through Ketamine Treatment isn't always linear.

The Path Forward; Actualizing & Exploring the Potential for Change

"I walk down the street. There is a deep hole in the sidewalk. I fall in. I am lost... I am helpless. It is not my fault. It takes forever to find a way out. I walk down the same street. There is a deep hole in the sidewalk. I pretend I do not see it. I fall in again. I can't believe I am in the same place. But it isn't my fault. It still takes me a long time to get out. I walk down the same street. There is a deep hole in the sidewalk. I see it is there. I still fall in. It is a habit. My eyes are open. I know where I am. It is my fault. I get out immediately. I walk down the same street. There is a deep hole in the sidewalk. I walk around it. I walk down another street." [1]

As we journey through this thing called life, we naturally come across challenging times that confuse and overwhelm us. Sometimes we successfully navigate the challenges, but other times we stumble and fall. Regardless of how it happens or how often, falling is painful. Even if we stay alert at all times, we can still fall. Fear and pain are unavoidable in this life, and we can't eliminate them completely, but we can minimize the time we spend on the ground by waking up to our patterns.

When we "wake up" to the habitual patterns that keep us walking the same road while expecting something new to happen, our suffering can be lessened. But how do we know if we are asleep?

Key signs signifying that you have not yet woken up include:

- Thoughts focused on blaming others
- Feeling victimized or powerless
- Reacting to challenges instead of responding

Ketamine Treatment can support the process of waking up, identifying, and examining our inner resources rather than being stuck in an endless pattern. In this chapter, we'll discuss how the awareness of our choices (whether we're awake or not) affects our outlook on and relationship to life, along with how Ketamine Treatment comes into play.

LEARNED HELPLESSNESS

What does it mean when you keep finding yourself reacting to challenges in the same way but expecting a different outcome? It means you've learned to be helpless. Because of your Rigid Ego, you cannot see the patterns that pull you down from your adaptable, true self. Ignoring these challenges and repeating patterns is not taking responsibility for change; it's allowing your suffering to be a dependable familiarity. The harsh truth is that unhappiness reflects where you are; it's a message that you must attempt to seek more and go deeper within yourself.

Still, who wants to hear that their dissatisfaction with life is of their own doing? Who wants to believe that their own decision making is what keeps them stuck? Who wants to know that you can't control the behaviors of others? No one! However, honesty with yourself, your Ego, and your role in your healing is necessary before entering Ketamine Treatment (which is why we have provided tools to identify your Ego level/stage). While the rigid internal guidance system is sustained by the belief that it keeps you safe from pain and harm, the system is, in fact, often the *source* of pain and hurt because it perpetuates these unhealthy patterns (like walking down the same path and falling in the same place).

Nonetheless, if you've reached this part of the book and recognize learned helplessness in yourself, please know this is a transitional moment and you are on the path to change. As the Dalai Lama once said, "Pain in life is not optional, but suffering is."[2] It's no surprise that life is hard and sometimes filled with pain, but it may be new to you to consider that suffering is optional.

You may ask: "How do I end this cycle? How do I free myself from suffering?"

You may end this cycle by "waking up," seeing something different for yourself, and knowing change is possible. Ketamine Treatment offers the unique perspective of finding hope within. This shift in perspective starts with you choosing to take accountability for your own happiness.

Taking accountability means thanking your Rigid Ego for protecting you to this point, but also telling it that it's not helping you see life fully and that another part will be in the driver's seat from now on. While you may feel protected by this Rigid Ego system of hypervigilance and threat detection, recognize that it's lessening your conscious awareness of the need for change and access to your inner resources. Your security and sense of stability are woven into the Rigid Ego system that maintains the status quo at your expense.

Building a Rigid Ego comes at the expense of abandoning other Ego resources that are part of your healthier side of self. It's an impoverished state where only a small portion of who you are and the gifts you possess function as if they are the whole.

Believing that change is possible is key. Ketamine Treatment can show you this system and its functions, which will take the power away from the Rigid Ego. This treatment shows you what has become invisible. As the molecule interacts with your neurology, it dissociates you from the control of the Rigid Ego while simultaneously allowing association with a healthier and more fluid Ego, leading you closer to your Essential Self. Doing so opens the door to seeing and experiencing more of who you are without constantly being on guard. Ketamine facilitates seeing the entirety of who you are and what your life can be, issuing an invitation to return to this perspective. Then, the KAS process helps in putting back together the whole of who you are as a unique person.

ENNEAGRAM PERSONALITY

To introduce how Ketamine and KAS assist in this process of seeing beyond what is familiar to self, we would like to provide an overview of the Enneagram Assessment.

The Enneagram is an ancient tool used throughout history and influenced by many different religious and spiritual traditions.[3] It synthesizes universal wisdom and philosophies from Christian, Jewish (especially the Kabbalah), Buddhist, and Muslim traditions into a map of nine fundamental personality types and complex intra/interpersonal relationships. The Enneagram is a tool to promote the value of self-reflection—from "waking up" to "paying attention to." It is a map that facilitates a deeper understanding and the ability to observe the role and functioning of the Rigid Ego and how it may limit us in exploring change and possibility.

The Enneagram breaks down human beings into nine distinct expressions of personality:[4]

1. The Reformer
2. The Helper
3. The Achiever
4. The Individualist
5. The Investigator
6. The Loyalist
7. The Enthusiast
8. The Challenger
9. The Peacemaker

The Enneagram, like this book, identifies personality as a synonym for Protective Ego Functioning. Personality is not who we are; it's the template for how we protect ourselves. Much like actors in a play, our personality functions as a role we develop and act out across time on the stage of life. Our role becomes confused with the actor when we become so committed to the familiarity of the role that we stop exploring new opportunities. Then, our Protective Ego Functioning becomes a place where we are limited in our emotions, thoughts, and behavior patterns. The Enneagram helps us better understand others in our preferred and most comfortable role, but it also emphasizes that determining our identity can improve awareness for change. We can control our own perception and ability to adapt by studying and understanding ourselves.

Enneagram Nomenclature Relating to Transformational Change		
Personality	VERSUS	Personal Essence
Asleep	VERSUS	Awake
Ego	VERSUS	Observing Self

Healthy	1. Level of Liberation 2. Level of Psychological Capacity 3. Level of Social Gift
Average	1. Level of Fixation 2. Level of Interpersonal Conflict 3. Level of Overcompensation
Unhealthy	1. Level of Violation 2. Level of Delusion and Compulsion 3. Level of Pathological Destructiveness

The Enneagram Levels focus on self-observation, where we become skilled at observing ourselves and our tendencies to respond or react as though we were watching someone else. When we observe ourselves, that means we see but do not internalize what's observed. The

Enneagram Levels identify nine types of observation with nine levels of health: three healthy, three average, and three unhealthy types in a dynamic model of integration and disintegration.[4] Can you identify your level?

Movement between the levels is facilitated by lessening the Rigid Ego's control and finding greater bandwidth to explore healthier intra/interpersonal orientation through self-awareness. The further we move down the levels, the more identified we are with the agenda of our Rigid Ego and the suffering we are holding onto. The higher we align with the levels, the more freedom and liberation we experience. Our capacity to have greater access to who we truly are is limited by our capacity for self-observation.

One of the crucial skills the Enneagram encourages us to acquire, which can be facilitated by Ketamine Treatment, is the ability to "observe and let go" of habitual patterns that keep the Rigid Ego in control and restrict us from the freedom to change. Letting go improves the capacity for self-observation and accessing the power to respond, rather than react, and resisting the temptation to continue with your habitual patterns. Don Riso and Russ Hudson capture this opening of the heart in the Wisdom of the Enneagram:[4]

"As we learn to be present to our lives and open to
the moment, miracles begin to happen.
One of the greatest miracles is that we can drop
a habit that has plagued us for many
years in a minute. When we are fully present the old habits let go, and we
are no longer the same. To experience the healing
of our oldest and deepest wounds
through the action of awareness is the miracle we
can all count on. If we follow this map
of the soul into the depths of our hearts, hatred will turn into compassion,
rejection into acceptance and fear into wonder."

WAKING UP

Always remember: there is so much more to who you are than what your limiting Rigid Ego will allow you to remember and is mistaking your identity for. Your Rigid Ego is accepting and believing that its limiting function is the *whole* Ego.

The road back to you begins with one step. This first step is waking up to the reality of your life beyond the Rigid Ego. It is opening the door, pushing past the Rigid Ego, and uncovering your ongoing tendencies.

Seeing life as it truly is is certainly an acquired taste. At times, life's bitterness can be overwhelming. It's quite natural to not want to see or look too closely into ourselves because we know that if we do, we might have to change, and change can feel scary! Transformational change could cause us to lose control over our delicately constructed life. We fear that if we look beneath the surface and welcome change, our so-called normal life will reveal itself as a cell of unhappiness that freedom is trapped in.

The Enneagram's teachings provide a map to guide you on this pilgrimage back to who you most deeply are which requires courage and bravery that will be needed during the Ketamine Treatment experience. Paying attention, seeing, and waking up depends solely on the amount of truth you can tolerate without retreating into your safe cell of the familiar.

Can you be brave enough to challenge your own limited and constructed Rigid Ego, knowing that it has been partially built for stability, protection, and meaning? Can you allow your Rigid Ego to move aside, opening your eyes to see how you are a player in your own suffering? How ready are you to go through the looking glass of your life, to tolerate the new and unfamiliar, to endure the surrendering to many things limiting your joy and fullness?

How do you know if you're ready? You are ready if you believe exploring the deeper side of self can provide expanded awareness and lead to readiness for transformational change.

Time spent exploring deep within ourselves, seeking different potential paths of health and happiness, is an investment in ourselves that we may need more time or encouragement to invest in. You are a worthy investment!

Paying attention to thoughts, actions, moods, and the ongoing inner self-dialogue just below the surface of awareness can be challenging to access. We seldom take the time or have the tools to look within while asking the most challenging questions without support and guidance. This kind of attention requires developing the buried parts of who "I" am and what is "true". This focus is difficult to achieve at first because the Rigid Ego is a master of disguise; its job is to create the illusion of change while keeping us "safe" in our chamber of security.

As discussed earlier, encounters with life's harshness can wake us up, but the Rigid Ego will try to keep this only as a momentary experience. The Rigid Ego returns as soon as possible to control, limit and filter what was experienced. It jumps in to blunt the full impact of seeing what the limited Ego cannot contain. But if we can endure the discomfort, the Rigid Ego's distortions can fade, and new opportunities for living life more fully emerge.

The goal of Ketamine Treatment is not to eliminate conscious or unconscious memory of our emotional connection to adverse/traumatic events (as if that were possible). Rather, the goal is to connect with the infinite depth of bravery, resilience, and courage that lies within your being. It's the ability to unwind from trauma, find space to feel mindful, and connect with the passion of aspirational living. This level of transformational change begins and ends with the realization that you have the power of choice. This realized power decides your internal functioning and guides the decisions that define your life each and every day.

Contrary to popular culture's insistence on "personal growth" as the key to mental wellness, the Ketamine Treatment path has a foundational belief that you have an inner healer already inside of you that has always been there.

ACTUALIZING CHANGE AS A RESULT OF KETAMINE TREATMENT

Ketamine Treatment is a unique experience that can ignite the exploration of lifestyle changes. Professional support during and post-treatment is crucial to integrate change into normal life. We encourage you to consider the value of counseling or coaching care to continue utilizing Ketamine Treatment as an available reset after your initial round of treatment. With the medication, you may find you have an effective tool to return to if faced again with your Rigid Ego and old habits of unhealthy thinking, emotion, or behavior begin to creep back in. As you move through this journey, you gain access to lessons that become easier with practice, and your ability to drive and direct the experience improves over time. The following list compiles lifestyle variables that you can expand upon as you find deeper and more meaningful connections with self and others:

- Expectations for intimacy and love
- Spiritual growth and connection
- Role as parent or caretaker
- Family connection and involvement
- Healthy routine to promote social connection
- Travel and new environment exploration
- Goals and aspirations
- Companionship and meaningful friendship connection
- Comfort in place of residence
- Financial security and lifestyle aspiration
- Vocational identity and job satisfaction
- Health and fitness
- Continued education, creativity, or self-expression
- Hobbies and recreation

Ketamine Treatment may open thoughts and exploration about what in life has become too familiar, and with access to the more adaptable and Fluid Ego, change will become a reality. Reflecting on

Adlerian Theory (humans are social beings), there exists a practical side to Ketamine personal development and growth work that involves striving for goals related to the vision you hold of your "ideal self."[5] Think of this as reclaiming superiority within yourself—taking the reins on your own life.

Ketamine Treatment can facilitate the exploration of your abandoned or ignored unconscious personal awareness. Through years of adapting to the new normal as you age, assuming responsibility often involves responsibility for others first. Your potential conscious awakening to life and living frees burdens of anxiety, depression, or habitual, self-defeating thinking patterns and offers a refocus on what's important. This is not abandoning responsibilities or others but remembering and reflecting on who you are and choose to be. Thoughts of the future and reclaiming a healthier version of ourselves create the re-instilling sense of hope we all deserve and desire. Remembering Ketamine Treatment is about change, we encourage you to expect and embrace the possibility of change to help you find the best version of you.

PART II

Welcome to Ketamine Treatment

4

Steps Involved in Ketamine Treatment (Preparation & Support)

KETAMINE CLINIC RECEPTION STAFF OBSERVATION/REFLECTION:
Having the opportunity to observe Ketamine clients on a weekly basis, I have noticed a change in our level of interaction, confidence in their presenting self, and transformation of the person that first entered our doors—it is unmistakable.

Let's circle back to the foundation of this journey. As we've discussed, the Rigid Ego patterns of worry, negative feelings, and intrusive hopelessness don't change in an instant, so Ketamine Treatment is no quick fix. Because of these facts, there are steps in the Ketamine process for unlocking your unrecognized potential for change and movement into transformation. This journey involves a deeper level of personal reflection outside of your familiar clouded thinking and remembering. External support and actively tracking your progress helps lift that cloud for clearer awareness.

In this chapter, we will more thoroughly review the Ketamine Treatment process with Ketamine Assisted Support (KAS) and the

Common Ketamine Progression Narrative (C-KPN) frameworks that we follow at Attento Counseling Practice. At Attento, we value Ketamine as an agent of change that can positively affect the intrapersonal, interpersonal, and lifestyle functioning. Depending on your treatment provider, they may use some or all of the framework we advocate for. Regardless of this presence, the medication's benefit to relieve symptoms of depression or anxiety is still there. However, the opportunity to ponder and fully actualize the transformational potential may not be achieved without support.

You are an active participant in this journey, and you can take full advantage of your Ketamine Treatment experience by seeking out understanding and self exploration along the way. Support can be provided as part of the Ketamine session experience or separate from the treatment day. If KAS integration sessions are not part of the Ketamine administration session itself, we recommend that integration happens as close to the time of the session as possible.

Although we strongly encourage you to find and engage a support team in the work you are doing, we also support you in doing it on your own with this guide. If that is your decision, then this book will assist you in the self-reflective work strategies to get more than just symptom relief from your treatment experience.

KETAMINE ASSISTED SUPPORT (KAS)

CLIENT REFLECTION:

Scared, concerned, and confused, I began my Ketamine Treatment experience through learning that eased my fears. My support team was available to guide me, ensure my safety, and help me make sense of this incredible experience that opened doors to deeper understanding. For the first time after years of therapy and endless hours of self-help work, the Ketamine experience moved me from coping to knowing.

The Ketamine Treatment experience with KAS involves your care team's guidance through every phase of support. Since the support relationship is directly influenced by the Ketamine experience, it is in no way, shape, or form like traditional therapy or coaching—meaning there is an opportunity for a very different level of connection. Instead of taking weeks or months to establish a trusting therapeutic or coaching connection, Ketamine Treatment with KAS offers the opportunity for a compression effect—the shortening of the time needed to establish a supportive alliance. This effect happens because you and the KAS professionals are present through the observable changes that happen in real time.

The work of the Multidisciplinary Association for Psychedelic Study (MAPS 2015 Assisted Psychotherapy Manual) has outlined the best practices for support through the Ketamine Treatment process.[1] Using these protocol recommendations, we have highlighted important steps and opportunities in this process. The KAS process constructs a healthy and individualized Ketamine Treatment routine to ensure each experience has the potential for meaningful exploration and healing. The predictability of a mutually agreed upon routine is essential to making the experience yours. Think of it as practicing for a play or a sports game. As you play or perform more often, the familiarity with the game or performance becomes more and more familiar and natural, even though each game or performance is different.

KAS intervention protocols continue to evolve and develop as this groundbreaking treatment for depression, anxiety, and PTSD continues to be researched. The following charts outline the process of Ketamine Treatment from a support perspective, pre-treatment to post-treatment, and best practices known at this time.

PRE-TREATMENT SUPPORT (INTAKE):

Psycho-education awareness and assessment of medical appropriateness to prepare for treatment. *Safety and appropriateness of Ketamine Treatment are paramount in this phase. The following should be reviewed as part of formal intake:*

1. Review the cost of treatment and Standard Practice Protocol for administration.

2. Review Informed Consent for Ketamine Services (full disclosure of treatment protocols, risks, alternative interventions; expectations for services, rights, and responsibilities).

PRE-TREATMENT SUPPORT (SETTING):

Preparation for the healing process; client-centric set & setting for Ketamine Treatment. *Provide a professional treatment space designed to support Ketamine Treatment. For certain providers, home-based treatment options may be considered and guidance for appropriate set and setting should be provided. Appropriateness in setting may include the following:*

1. Space to recline or lay, headphones, external music options in support of the experience, eye mask, blankets or pillows for comfort, and low lighting.

2. Confirmation of access to personal safety-related support is available as needed.

3. As appropriate, non-intrusive medical monitoring to ensure safety.

4. Ensured awareness of emergency contact and required driver/transportation arrangements post-treatment if receiving services at practice or clinic (normal protocol is no driving post treatment for remainder of the day).

5. Establish setting or pre-treatment routines for client comfort.

PRE-TREATMENT SUPPORT (SESSION PREPARATION):
FIRST TREATMENT: Discussion of the current level of functioning, ensuring readiness, awareness, and expectation for treatment.
CONTINUATION TREATMENT: Processing of recent post-treatment experience before the Ketamine experience continuation session.

The following is a list of specific items that may be reviewed in the process of check-in:

1. Confirm pre-session commitment to adhering to MD instructions on the day of treatment.

    • Appropriate medication management on the day of treatment.
    • Sobriety on treatment day and evening prior.
    • Pre-session 4-hour fasting.

2. Prepare for the session by reviewing possible post-treatment side effects (light headache, nausea, brain fog, emotional lability, anxiety spike), discuss and establish support by confirming MD or KAS Specialist availability for support.

3. Confirmation of time availability for treatment session preparation, period of administration, processing and recovery (estimated 2-4 hours based on the form of administration).

4. Confirm client support to be offered during the session (communication of steps and consent for possible grounding touch as needed).

5. A formal overview of expected Ketamine medication effect based on administration (onset/deeper experience level, transition from experience to coming out).

PRE-TREATMENT SUPPORT (SESSION FOCUS):
Ketamine experience intention setting:

1. Client-directed intention setting for the session: what the client would like to achieve as a result of experience.

   • Start simple—peace, mindfulness, letting go, exploring the new, etc.
   • Transition to more focused intention depending on the desire for deeper self-exploration.

2. Reminder of the presence of an observational voice that can assist with guiding or exploring an experience (voice can act as an inner healer supporting positive interpersonal dialogue).

3. Support understanding that the disassociation experience can support freedom/reset to possible re-association with a healthier side of self (letting go of Ego Rigidity).

TREATMENT SUPPORT (KETAMINE MEDICINE ADMINISTRATION):
During Ketamine Treatment experience:

1. Administration of medication via self-administered tabs following prescription/MD dosing guidelines, medical professional IV/IM infusion, or Nasal Administration.

2. Professional observation of initial effects of medication (5-15 minutes post administration), increase in dosing based on assessment (client verbal report related to the level of dissociative experience: light/moderate/deep).

3. Continued monitoring and support during treatment experience. Average time is 45 to 90 minutes based on the form of administration and client sensitivity.

4. Support person utilizes grounding techniques if the client experiences duress or needs support during the experience (clients normally respond to gentle shoulder, arm, hand touch, or verbal intervention assisting with movement out of deeper experience).

5. Guided support for client's return from experience—slow and gentle.

6. Observation and support during the period of mindfulness and recovery post-experience (5-15 minutes).

7. Appropriate dosing assessment.

POST-TREATMENT SUPPORT (IMMEDIATE OR DAYS FOLLOWING TREATMENT HEALING/REFLECTIVE PROCESSING POST TREATMENT):
Post Ketamine Treatment integration.

1. KAS Specialist or MD supported non-directive communication and reflection related to experience.

2. Processing of experience with client looking for themes, content, or emotional/physical reflections that allow access to the inner healer and create a healing anchor for the experience.

3. Assessment of predominant or transitional C-KPN Phase Level of Experience:
   PHASE 1: Past Period Person/Place Orientation
   PHASE 2: Exploration of Detachment/Deeper Level of Mindfulness
   PHASE 3: Exploration of Aspiration-Future Orientation
   (*Detailed overview of Ketamine experience Phases provided in chapter 2*).

4. Exploration of Ketamine medicine effect—reductions in symptoms of anxiety and/or depression.

5. Focus on healing integration—the link between experience and possibility of change—greater access to choice and emotional neutrality related to past adverse experiences.

6. Anchor experience progression to Common Ketamine Progression Narrative (C-KPN) to establish a language for discussion of change as a result of treatment.

7. Post-treatment recommendations for continued self-reflection/mindfulness (*reflection guide provided at the end of this book*).

POST-TREATMENT SUPPORT (AFTER-CARE & FOLLOW-UP CONNECTION):

Continued healing support after Ketamine Treatment.

1. Continued KAS/MD assessment of treatment effect and establishment of recommendations for continuation of care.

2. Post-treatment change of state assessment (use of C-KPN to explore change and improvement in functioning or other provider measurement/self-reflective strategies).

3. Exploration of client alternative mental wellness support practices—meditation, self-care commitment, and expanded social engagement.

4. Connection with support systems (therapy, family, and community).

Your Ketamine Treatment team will help you feel prepared, safe and supported during this time of expanded personal awareness. Unlike other psychedelics that utilize discussion and exploration of surroundings outside of self when under the influence of the medication (i.e., landscape, space, active verbal interaction), KAS focuses on supporting an internal experience—a deeper look at yourself supported by the observer(s). The healing nature of this support focuses on establishing a setting for self-reflection, internal work, and exploration. A therapist or specialist is a sounding board for processing the dissociative experience to foster a new level of personal insight and perspective in a process known as integration and anchoring. Your support specialist integrates and anchors moments so you can hold onto them, connect with them, and process them when the Ketamine administration experience comes to a natural close. New thinking, emotional availability, and self-awareness created by the experience offer the "window of opportunity" for exploration from which a long-term positive impact on personal perspective and functioning can emerge.

Talk therapy helps solidify the changes prompted by Ketamine by using the period of reduced anxiety and depression as a time for deeper exploration of potential long-term change. Psychotherapy and KAS open an opportunity for improvement in the four A's: Awareness, Acceptance, Appreciation, and Awakening. Consider the four A's from this perspective:

> **The experience of trauma can leave a long-term negative emotional impact on our person. Ketamine Treatment can achieve a similar result in the opposite direction by leaving a long-term positive impact on our presenting person through awareness of our incredible capacity for change.**

The richness of the multi-dimensional experience requires time for processing and contemplation. Unique to Ketamine intervention is that every Ketamine Treatment is different in content and interpersonal experience. This experiential property of the experience is often new and can be overwhelming, but it is a wonderful dimension of self-healing that you first experience and then process. Although there are certain aspects of the Ketamine experience that are beyond the scope of simple explanation, there is no need to worry. You will not be alone in your experience. Ask questions, investigate, and become an informed consumer of Ketamine. Above all, hold on to the expectation that progress and change are possible. Your care team's priority is to make sure you benefit from treatment.

COMMON KETAMINE PROGRESSION NARRATIVE (C-KPN)

A Ketamine Treatment foundational belief, based on research and experience, is that there is potential for lessening symptoms to improve general functioning, even for those with treatment-resistant anxiety or depression. The C-KPN framework offers meaningful pre-session intention setting to tackle self-reflective processing post-session; it is a treatment-specific language for conceptualizing personal growth, transformation, and the pathway to getting there. These change areas have been introduced in earlier chapters; however, as we approach your Ketamine Treatment decision, we want to remind you of the support you have in your journey. In Ketamine work, the psychological variables are the most challenging to identify. Ketamine Treatment experiences are often filled with diverse content, feelings, and reflections. Understanding the psychological areas of change and expanded awareness guides you in finding meaning through the experience beyond anxiety or depression symptom reduction.

In the table below, we identify and define areas for measuring change. Moving through desired change is a journey, not a destination, so it may take time. As a result of treatment, you'll have the opportunity for more focused healing, and with your support team, you can discover healthier paths for change post-treatment.

AREAS FOR POTENTIAL CHANGE

Potential Area of Symptom Change	C-KPN Progression: What Could Change Due to Ketamine Treatment
Baseline Depression/ Anxiety Reduction	Feeling lesser symptoms of depression or anxiety and improvement of lifestyle functioning and social engagement.
Potential Areas of Psychological Change	C-KPN Progression: What Could Change Due to Ketamine Treatment
Development of Ego Level (Fluidity vs. Rigidity)	Potential to explore growth and wellness through Ego awareness.
Ego Stage (Flexibility & Resilience)	Availability of a more positive personal orientation to an event or experience.

Adverse Childhood Experience (ACE) and/or Significant Life Traumatic Event(s) Impacting Lifestyle Functioning	Potential to unwind from traumatic experiences as a result of exploring greater emotional neutrality.
Personality Orientation	Recognition, awareness, and relationship acceptance with Authentic and Essential Self.
Ketamine Phase Progression: Comfort and Processing in the Experience	Access to the inner healer, lessening the impact of the Rigid Ego, and having the ability to experience deeper feelings of mindfulness and aspiration.
Self-Medication– Substance Use or Dependence (unhealthy coping strategies to self-manage depression, anxiety, PTSD)	Potential to explore healthier coping.

This framework maps out the changes in symptoms, thinking, emotional, and behavioral tendencies that may result from Ketamine Treatment. These areas of change also reviewed in Chapter 2 are not exhaustive, but they offer a starting place to reflect on how a support team may evaluate your progress. We encourage you to be familiar with the C-KPN concept of transformational change to facilitate movement into a stronger position of ownership of your treatment and mental wellness endeavors. Keep it simple and focus on understandable concepts that feel comfortable and are important to you.

REFLECT ON THIS QUESTION AFTER REVIEWING THE CHART ABOVE:
*Based on what I've learned so far, how might
Ketamine Treatment help me?*

CLIENT REFLECTIONS
Take a glimpse into the varied and profound client experiences through a few quotes we've collected. These are actual comments shared by real clients within our practice during and post their Ketamine experiences:

"I saw my younger self and reconnected with my old nickname Smiley; I want to get to know that person again."
(First session post-experience reflection: Female, 32).

"With 5 years of devoted work meditating daily, I followed my practice steps to move into the experience but tumbled backward and realized I had to let go and fall into a more peaceful place."
(Third session post-experience reflection: Male, 39).

"Why the F did you make me do this?!"
(During experience sharing: Female, 51)
This client elected to continue 10 more treatments showing successive progress in both comfort with experience and changes in functioning.

"I was embraced by my God; that is all I have to share at this time."
(Second session post-experience reflection: Female, 54)

"It was not unpleasant; I have no words to describe it."
(First session post-experience reflection: Female, 72).

"I have struggled with this my whole life. I finally figured it out: it's about a contract, a contract that binds me to give my love to others."
(During second session integration: Male, 46).

"It was dark and uncomfortable, but I got through it. I am not sure what to do with this; something meaningful has happened."
(First session post-experience reflection: Female, 31).

"For the first time in my life, I felt separation from my resentment and regret."
(Fourth session post-experience reflection: Male, 50).

"It was like being shot out of a cannon, I moved outside of myself and saw so many possibilities."
(First session post-experience reflection: Male, 39).

As you can gather from these client reflections, Ketamine Treatment opens a very unique and individualized window of opportunity to look for new paths toward insightful self-reflection. We cannot determine your path—you must trust your inner healer and support team to guide you.

Ketamine work is often the most interesting, immediate, and in many cases, enjoyable healing work you can embark on. We are all capable of change in our pursuit of being the best version of ourselves. A brief time-out from your normal can be an opportunity to explore a stronger version of you.

KETAMINE TREATMENT OPTIONS

The methods for delivering Ketamine Treatment often determine the availability and access to therapeutic or coaching KAS; many Ketamine Treatment clinics or practices offer multiple administration forms and access. We recommend finding your right fit and actively planning support outside of direct administration. The following chart exhibits how treatment differs across provider types:

Forms of Administration:	Therapeutic/Coaching KAS Support Expectation:	Possible Path for Support:
Tab-based Prescription (Home-based)	Guided online KAS (therapist or specialist)	Involvement of current or new therapist/specialist in home-based treatment work processing pre and post session
Tab-based Prescription (KAS Practice)	Integration of KAS with prescription management from a psychiatrist	Therapist/KAS specialist as an essential component of Ketamine Treatment experience

Intravenous (IV) Clinic	Transactional model of Ketamine delivered	Possible assignment to in or out of office therapist/specialist, most often offered on a different day than Ketamine dosing
Intravenous (IV) Therapy Practice	KAS available; sometimes paired with Ketamine dosing	Possible involvement of current or new therapist/specialist in IV clinic during or after Ketamine Treatment
Nasal Clinic	Transactional model of Ketamine delivered	Possible assignment to in or out of office therapist/specialist, most often offered on a different day than Ketamine dosing
Intramuscular Therapy Clinic	KAS available; sometimes paired with Ketamine dosing	Medical professional providing direct therapeutic and administration support for experience; possible joint work with therapist/specialist.

As Ketamine Treatment grows in popularity, the types of tools used to track client progress continue to expand. With the new wave of technology integration into healthcare, many clinics, therapists, and specialists can use software to assess, document, and track treatment progress. Apps and daily tracker tools can also support self-reflection and measure psychological change. Similar to treatment sessions, this tracking work promotes expanded self-awareness and change potential. These tools are in their infancy and are becoming increasingly easier to use.

However, these tools are not required for ongoing awareness and discussion related to treatment progression. As you voyage through Ketamine Treatment, we recommend you consider, regardless of your form of administration (IV, IM, Tabs, Nasal) whether the treatment environment provides access to optimal services that will allow you to take full advantage of your Ketamine experience. By owning your Ketamine Treatment decision, you are in a remarkable position to find the most useful resources that will support you in your work.

REMEMBER...

An infamous quote hangs outside many therapists' offices:

"Lasting change begins outside the door of this office."

5

Understanding the Healing Perspective, Mechanism of Action: Ketamine Medicine Effect

CLIENT REFLECTION:
As I exited my first treatment, I felt a level of calm that I had not felt in the past 30 years. I remembered what it felt like to live without this tremendous weight I had been carrying for years.

It's all too common for individuals diagnosed with anxiety or depression to not find solutions in conventional treatment. In fact, 35% of people diagnosed with depression or anxiety disorders are treatment-resistant to traditional forms of anxiety or depression symptom reduction.[1]

So how is "treatment-resistant" characterized, and how does it relate to Ketamine? Treatment-resistant anxiety and/or depression means having persistent symptoms despite two (2) or more forms of intervention, including medications and therapy. As one of the most well-researched medications on the market, the FDA recognizes Ketamine treatment for those who have tried two other forms of treatment and continue to experience symptoms.

In this chapter, we'll take a step back and discuss the big picture of Ketamine: history, mechanism of action (how it works), side effects, and addiction. When you are evaluated for Ketamine Treatment, you'll learn even more about how these topics relate to you as an appropriate candidate for treatment. For now, we're speaking in general terms.

KETAMINE'S HISTORY

After the wave of new anesthetic drugs in the 1950s and 1960s, Ketamine was first produced in 1962 to reduce the unpleasant side effects of related compounds.[2] Eight years later, in 1970, the first use of Ketamine outside of a laboratory or clinical trial took place. Then, after decades of being used as a sedative, the FDA approved Ketamine in 2019 for use in anxiety and depression treatment as a nasal spray under the brand name Spravato.[3] This approval means that Ketamine can be safely used, with proper medical and support supervision, as a sub-sedative (not inducing a full sleep state) agent for treating treatment-resistant anxiety and depression.[4]

Although Ketamine is currently (as of this book publication, 2023) FDA-approved only as Spravato nasal spray, the future is bright for Ketamine Treatment; continued research is expected to support the approval of additional forms of administration. Other forms of Ketamine administration (tabs, intravenous (IV), and intramuscular (IM)) are prescribed as off-label treatments not yet approved by the FDA.

KETAMINE'S INTERACTION WITH YOUR BRAIN

Ketamine interacts with several chemical receptors in your body's nervous system that are related to the brain-based changes brought about by treatment. These receptors are protein-based structures on the surface of nerve cells that cause downstream effects when stimulated by certain molecules. During treatment, Ketamine blocks the NMDA (N-methyl-D-aspartate) receptor, which is essential for learning and memory.[5] This blocked NMDA receptor is the reason for the dissociative effect of Ketamine, which is the mechanism of action that adds antidepressant effects and establishes new connections between neurons (defined earlier as an increased neural plasticity). Ketamine also affects the AMPA receptor, which is responsible for short-term brain change. Modifying this receptor may play a role in Ketamine's antidepressant effects.[6] Ketamine also reduces physical and psychological pain through a variety of mechanisms.

KETAMINE'S INTERACTION WITH YOUR BODY

Ketamine also affects other body systems, such as increasing your blood pressure and heart rate in your cardiovascular system during treatment. Because Ketamine affects your heart, your MD will complete an evaluation to ensure safety with the medication (this happens during Ketamine Treatment appropriateness at the time of intake before the initial treatment session). The evaluation involves the determination of normal blood pressure, if medication is being used to manage blood pressure, and understanding of prior cardiac related treatment or conditions. During treatment, changes in blood pressure and heart rate are temporary and return to normal within a few hours.[7] The focus of the pre-treatment MD cardiac evaluation is to determine safety during treatment when blood can be affected.

KETAMINE'S POTENTIAL SIDE EFFECTS

The following is a list of the most common side effects of Ketamine administration[8]:

- Nausea and vomiting
- Dizziness, double vision
- Dysphoria (dissatisfaction or unhappiness)
- Confusion
- Drowsiness

Having said this, these side effects are mild, don't last long, and aren't common. But, if you were to experience these effects, your treatment team is adequately trained to support you.

More serious side effects of Ketamine include allergic reactions, seizures, muscle stiffness, and abnormal heart rhythms. However, these effects of Ketamine are rare because thorough pre-treatment medical screening minimizes the risk of these more serious complications.

KETAMINE TREATMENT CONTRAINDICATIONS

The following is a list of medical condition concerns (contraindications) that require evaluation to determine if Ketamine Treatment is appropriate for you:

- Uncontrolled coronary artery disease (heart disease)
- Uncontrolled hypertension (high blood pressure)
- Increased blood pressure and heart rate (this increased strain could lead to chest pain or even a heart attack)
- High thyroid hormone levels (can increase blood pressure and risk of heart-related complications)
- Compromised or non-normal liver functioning
- Allergic reaction to Ketamine (would exclude you from treatment)

This is not an exhaustive list of contraindications to Ketamine Treatment. In preparing for Ketamine Treatment, an MD will provide a formal examination to determine if Ketamine is a safe option for your treatment path.

KETAMINE ADDICTION

In addition to direct treatment side effects, you may be wondering, like many clients do, about the possible addictive nature of Ketamine Treatment.[9] Unlike other psychiatric medications used mostly to treat anxiety, Ketamine does not work on the opioid centers of the brain, which is the area of the brain that has a greater potential to create dependency or physical craving. The potential of Ketamine addiction is viewed as relatively low, sitting in the mid-range of addictive potential above cannabis.

Instead, Ketamine is similar to other psychedelics like psilocybin and ibogaine, which have current research suggesting that they may actually be useful (under proper medical supervision) in treating addiction. However, with this being said, Ketamine, like any other drug, can be addictive and habit-forming based on a client's desire to chase a high or seek escapism.

Ketamine addiction is mostly observed in uncontrolled higher dosing, self-medication, and recreational use. Ketamine's property of emotional detachment drives the risk of misuse with self-medication and recreational use. Because of this risk, the best prevention against emotional dependence is a commitment to only using Ketamine with a qualified medical professional, not for self-medication or recreational use.

Appropriate low-level supervised clinical dosing has a long history of safe administration and outcomes. Your medical team will ensure that using Ketamine for mental wellness treatment is appropriate for you by screening for possible untreated substance abuse. During this time, appropriate safeguards, including not giving treatment approval, can be assessed to ensure safety and lessen the probability of medication dependence.

ROUTES OF ADMINISTRATION

There are several routes of administration for Ketamine. These include intravenous (IV), intramuscular (IM), oral (tabs), and intranasal. IV administration has the fastest onset of any route of administration; the drug reaches the brain in 1-2 minutes with IV administration. IM administration involves injecting Ketamine into the deltoid (shoulder muscle). This route also has a rapid onset but is slightly slower than IV administration, at about 3-5 minutes. In both of these administrations, Ketamine is injected as a liquid.

Another way to take Ketamine is through a dissolvable tablet or waxy troche (like a cough drop). These oral formulations dissolve under the tongue or between the tongue and cheek. Medication absorption occurs through blood vessels in the mouth. In this case, the effects of oral

Ketamine begin around 10-15 minutes into the experience. Absorption from the stomach contributes to the effects after swallowing the dissolved medication. The level of Ketamine session experience depends on individual absorption and sensitivity. Unlike IV or IM administration, time in experience using tablets or troches may be extended because it is based on absorption and the body's metabolizing the medication.

Lastly, Ketamine can be received through the nasal spray Spravato. Ketamine exists as two mirror-image molecules, and the intranasal drug is one of these molecules. Nasal sprays are fast-acting and usually have a distinct start similar to IV and IM administration and an end similar to tablets or troches (sometimes extended). Nasal administration can be uncomfortable for some, and managing the actual dosing level is sometimes challenging. Recent improvements in the spray applicator design has helped with both uptake and using these products.

THE KETAMINE TREATMENT ENVIRONMENT AND EXPERIENCE

The typical protocol for exploring the Ketamine Effect usually involves a commitment to an initial four Ketamine Treatment sessions. Usually administered in consecutive weekly sessions, the four Ketamine Treatment session experiences allow you and your support team to gradually gauge your appropriate level of comfortable dissociation based on level of dosing. The Ketamine experience is unique to each and every individual, so time is needed to determine the appropriate therapeutic dosing level and the resulting effect.

The Ketamine Treatment experience requires an environment that supports internal reflective work without outside distractions. Under sub-sedative dosing, there is ordinarily little verbal interaction during the experience. Since eyes become more sensitive to light during the experience, most clients wear an eye mask to have an internal experience without disturbance. We also encourage headphones to play music (usually spa, mindful, or ambient-type music selection) to block out surrounding sounds and add grounding and a sense of flow during the treatment experience.

Ketamine Treatment experience sessions are always evolving, so it's part of the therapeutic process to be open to the diverse content and ever-changing nature. While taking the medicine, clients often encounter ever-changing imagery and the sensation of floating, feeling disconnected from the body, tingling, or vibrating. Some clients describe the experience as out-of-body with an observational voice guiding and processing the experience. The Ketamine experience can even take on a spiritual dimension; many clients express a connection to nature or to a greater whole. The experience may be emotional, ranging from elation and euphoria to reflective sadness based on the content of your internal experience. In all the unpredictability, you can depend on the fact that the Ketamine experience content comes from within you.

The dissociative state naturally reduces 45 minutes to 1.5 hours after the start of treatment, and then you will return to more awareness of your physical body and surroundings. Unlike other more unpredictable "length of experience" psychedelics, Ketamine usually has a distinct start to the experience, a dissociative phase, and then a gradual return.

It's common for clients to struggle with letting go of a normal state of awareness and becoming comfortable with the dissociative effects of Ketamine. If this is difficult, look to your medical team and the C-KPN concepts for support. Repeated experiences with Ketamine will help you become more familiar with its effects and the feeling of dissociating. Remember, the dissociation from habituated Rigid Ego functioning facilitates the potential change and expanded awareness.

No matter what you experience, your KAS team will be there to guide you through anything you encounter, even darkness. Moving towards and through any unpleasant or negative emotions may seem scary, but with this support, it's therapeutic. Your KAS team will encourage you to actively observe thoughts and emotions and hold onto things of value as they transition. These thoughts and emotions are part of the therapeutic and reflective content you will dive into during the integration phase of the KAS process and through your individual work outside of treatment sessions.

The reduction in symptoms of anxiety and depression—the Ketamine Effect—is often experienced during and after treatment. These effects can last days or weeks, even though the medication itself will be processed through your body's physiology in 3-5 hours. Compared to the effects of traditional anxiety or depression medication, which can sometimes take 3-4 weeks, this more immediate symptom reduction is noteworthy. The longer-term decrease in anxiety and depression symptoms extends further with treatment continuation.

YOUR CURRENT MEDICATIONS FOR ANXIETY AND/OR DEPRESSION

If you are currently prescribed medication for anxiety or depression and are looking to stop taking them, you're like many others who enter Ketamine Treatment. Many clients enter into Ketamine Treatment with the desire to move away from the long-term use of antidepressants and other medications. These medications for depression and anxiety include selective serotonin reuptake inhibitors (SSRIs), serotonin norepinephrine reuptake inhibitors (SNRIs), tricyclic antidepressants (TCAs), and antipsychotics. Other anxiety medications are benzodiazepines, such as alprazolam, and the non-benzodiazepine buspirone. This is an understandable desire and goal for treatment. However, it is rarely a near-term option when considering the Ketamine treatment path.

When starting Ketamine Treatment, your medication for depression or anxiety will most likely be continued under the guidance of your prescribing psychiatrist or MD. Changing your prescribed medication will be discussed after you and your prescriber determine the effect of Ketamine Treatment for you. Please remember the treatment path is part of a journey, not the destination. Expect change and be prepared to follow guided steps to uncover an improved level of wellness.

REMEMBER...

- Ketamine is a well-researched medication with a long history of providing support for both medical intervention and psychiatric support.

- Ketamine is only FDA-approved in the psychiatric space as Spravato, the nasal spray. Trials are ongoing, and its broader use as an agent to treat treatment-resistant anxiety and depression is expected in the coming years.
- Medical professionals (psychiatrists or MDs) can prescribe Ketamine as an "off-label treatment" for anxiety and depression. This is a common practice.
- Ketamine is used specifically as an agent to foster a therapeutic experience and is not taken as a daily medication.
- The Ketamine Treatment dissociative timeline is an *experience* facilitating potential for symptom reduction and deeper healing. The support of a qualified and intensively trained medical team is essential to offer you support before, during, and after your Ketamine Treatment experience.
- Transition from your current support medication is possible. However, it usually happens over time under the supervision and guidance of your attending MD.

6

Making Your Ketamine Treatment Decision

CLIENT REFLECTION:
*I realized I was effectively coping, and it was exhausting.
I needed the change of a new year to convince myself
that my mental wellness needed to be first—everything else
should become second to this priority!*

At this point in our journey through the information provided in this book, you may be considering your Ketamine Treatment decision. We've taken you through the definition of treatment resistant anxiety and depression, Ego focused exploration, transformational change level work, C-KPN, your personality type, Ketamine mechanisms, treatment protocols, and the value of support. With all of this, we've continued to reiterate that your personal exploration and choice to enter a Ketamine Treatment discovery path is up to you. Your observations, processes, and internalizations will only be uncovered when the limiting control of the Rigid Ego is relaxed. Only then can you grasp the magnitude of potential transformation within.

With all that said, *do you still have concerns?*

Even with all the background information about how Ketamine works in the mind, body, and spirit, no person begins Ketamine Treatment without question or concern. This chapter will address your fear and uncertainty to equip you with the considerations you need to make your decision.

We'll address three common and understandable areas of concern:

- Your general thoughts about the psychedelic experience
- Your unhealthy coping strategies in relation to Ketamine treatment
- Your emotional processing tendency related to your personality type

CONCERN #1: PSYCHEDELIC EXPERIENCE

As a psychedelic agent, Ketamine produces an altered state of consciousness called dissociation. Feeling unsure about the psychedelic experience and your short-term and long-term control over it is normal. Stories of K-Holes and drifting with no return are largely related to unsupervised recreational use.

Yes, the experience is certainly unique if you've never taken psychedelics in the past. However, of the many psychedelics used either medically or recreationally, Ketamine is a gentler medication. Under the appropriate guidance, it can be safely administered and facilitate an internal return-to-self experience. You may already be familiar with altered states of consciousness (daydreaming, meditation, sleep, trying or using alcohol/marijuana); Ketamine is another one on the list. Remember, the experienced practitioner is trained to slowly introduce you to the dissociative state of Ketamine so you can experience the medication's perceptual effect before entering where it will ultimately take you.

WHAT DOES THE PSYCHEDELIC EFFECT ENTAIL?

Ketamine activates the brain with diverse experiences of memory, image, and feeling (for most).

Many clients describe:

- Detailed reflections of past events and experiences with emotional neutrality (observing the event or experience instead of feeling the familiar traumatic aspects of the experiences)
- Exploration of robust color and a multi-level experience with familiar and unfamiliar content
- An ever-transitioning experience of emotional and visual content
- Deep reflective thinking about past, current, and future perspectives
- Feeling a deep level of inner calm/mindfulness and absence of familiar symptoms of anxiety and/or depression
- Detachment to external physical body awareness with pain reduction (numbness)
- Greater connection to our innate potential for change
- Heightened awareness to essential aspects of self

Imagine the movie trailers that play before a film starts. They're presented briefly and change quickly, following a selected soundtrack. The Ketamine experience is similar: things enter, can be explored, observed, or felt. Then, there's a transition to another experience, which can be related, new, overlapping, or completely random. You'll observe a constant movement of exploration guided by your active inner voice. There is a need to surrender (picture yourself as a passenger in a car observing the scenery), but this does not mean you must fully give up awareness or consciousness.

Although Ketamine Treatment is a deeply internal experience with an unpredictable pattern, frequency, and depth, the presence of a support person means you can signal or request support at any point. Your guide will teach you simple grounding techniques that can easily pull you from or lessen the intensity of the experience as needed.

Most clients are quiet and non-verbal during the experience. Afterward, they often describe it as multidimensional, beyond words, and hard to adequately describe. Although we can find patterns in client experiences, each individual encounters something unique. Clients go into different depths of dissociation, and the effects of your treatment are not determined by how deep you go. Regardless of whether you experience high or low dissociation, Ketamine can profoundly affect persistent anxiety and depression by allowing you to identify the origin of your symptoms and make intentional changes. Beyond a dream-like state, the emotional connection to the experience can be very real and is often found to be intense, blissful, or freeing.

SHOULD I BE SCARED?

Familiarity with both the Ketamine Medication Effect and treatment process is a skill that is learned and developed through each individual's experience. You may feel anxiety before or during the first treatment, which is completely normal. The understandable feelings of concern diminish as you become more and more familiar with the experience, and your Ego begins to release its need to control. Your treatment team will assist you in being prepared for your first experience—breathe, relax, and invite in your most open self. With experience and practice, the ability to let go becomes easier.

**CONCERN #2: UNHEALTHY COPING STRATEGIES
AND KETAMINE TREATMENT READINESS**

Nobody enjoys emotional pain, and we each have different tolerances for how much we can take. Depending on your resistance to emotional pain, you may have searched for quick relief in maladaptive (unhealthy) coping mechanisms to distract or compensate for emotions that feel overwhelming. Having said that, unhealthy coping mechanisms are hardly ever worthwhile. Quick fixes leave as quickly as they come, and they turn your life into an endless chase for an ounce of relief. To live freely, you must have ups and downs; that is the beautiful fact of life!

**Are there any unhealthy coping mechanisms
you currently practice?**

Answering yes to this question doesn't make you a flawed or bad person. Many of us survive this way. But you must recognize that these coping mechanisms are your Rigid Ego compensating to ease pain, endure, cope, and repeat for protection. These coping strategies, while adaptive in the original context, become counterproductive across time. The good news is they are not permanent; they satisfy the security needs of the Rigid Ego but are not unchangeable. Dependence on unhealthy coping exacts a toll on ourselves and those around us.

To understand unhealthy coping and how it prevents exploration of deeper healing, it may be helpful to review the list of tendencies that suggest self-medication or compensation:

- Use of substances for emotional relief (alcohol, drugs)
- Self-indulgent behavior (gambling, emotional eating, excessive routine activity, workaholic behavior, sex preoccupation)
- Isolation (living through social media, gaming dependence, excessive sleeping)
- Codependency (drama, excessive care for others)

Ask yourself:

- Do I see a pattern of behavior?
- What is my *true motivation* behind my behavior?

Understanding the fine line between dependence on these tendencies and the ability to choose to stop is essential for understanding if unhealthy tendencies exist in your life or define your life.

Ask yourself: Does the behavior control me, or do I control the behavior?

HOW DOES UNHEALTHY COPING RELATE TO KETAMINE TREATMENT?
Preparing for Ketamine Treatment involves reflecting on your unhealthy

coping mechanisms and committing yourself to move outside of them. Ketamine may decrease your cravings and dependence on old coping patterns and highlight the temporary nature of self-medication from the pain.[1] This change will reform your behavior and lifestyle, and you may feel a loss of familiarity with that previous version of yourself. But this loss is necessary for you to move forward into healing. Moving outside of the familiar offers an opportunity for new strategies regarding need, dependence, and what is healthy. Take a moment, sit back, and think about your Ketamine Treatment decision.

Can you recognize a history of coping that has let you keep a safe distance from doing deeper work? Can you let go of that coping to enter the healing power of Ketamine Treatment?

CONCERN #3: EMOTIONAL PROCESSING RELATED TO A NEW PATH OF TREATMENT

When considering Ketamine Treatment and the experience of a sub-sedative psychedelic experience, ask yourself:

What is my ability to let go and embrace new experiences?

We all interact with our lives from a personality based on our habitual thoughts, emotions, and behavioral responses. Reflect on what you learned about personality; it is how we protect ourselves from unknown risks associated with new experiences. Understanding how your personality processes the newness of Ketamine Treatment can help you personalize preparation to lessen anxiety.

Remember the Enneagram from Chapter 3? Use the following chart derived from the Enneagram Triad Centers to identify your dominant initial response when thinking about the unfamiliarity of Ketamine Treatment:[2]

Prominent First Feeling When Considering Uniqueness of Ketamine Treatment:	Feeling Orientation Center (emotional processing center):	Action Needed to Ease Concerns & Answer Questions:
Fear/Anxiety	Thinking/Head	Accessing information and resources to promote deeper understanding and feelings of **security** (Ex: This book, web search, reading, gathering information/ data from your Ketamine support team).
Immediate Resistant Response	Instinctive/Gut	Seeking direct support to change the gut feeling about the experience. Interacting with people who have had Ketamine Treatment experiences to flip the switch from resistance to **acceptance and commitment**.
Worry/Shame/ Uncertainty	Feeling/Heart	Looking for emotional support to provide **validation** and **understanding**. Needing to understand how the treatment option is related to personal growth and a more positive self-identity.

Pause and feel your natural personality type inclination. Know that it is expected. You can move forward by taking action to ease your concerns. Getting through the initial step of experiencing the first treatment is by far the most challenging but the most important. The ability to take this first step opens the "window of opportunity" to determine if the Ketamine Treatment option aligns with you.

MOVING FORWARD

Given the experiential nature of Ketamine treatment, we recognize your concern and desire for more knowledge as you plan to potentially move forward. We encourage you to use this information to evaluate how to become a better-informed potential client. At this point, overcoming fear is the greatest challenge in finding the strength to take a step in a new direction. We recommend you sincerely attempt to cultivate positive and aspirational feelings about your potential transformation through Ketamine intervention and have realistic expectations along with readiness to do the work.

The following questions may also assist you in evaluating your readiness for Ketamine Treatment:

- Is my anxiety and/or depression treatment-resistant?
- Can I recognize a traumatic life experience or series of moments that may make me a good candidate for Ketamine Treatment?
- Do I recognize the unhealthy patterns of coping that have become disruptive and limiting in my life?
- Do I believe in transformational change?
- Do I recognize Ketamine treatment begins with my understanding that the Rigid Ego is just a part of a much broader resource that can be discovered through this work?
- Do I trust the professionals and Ketamine experience as an endeavor with a solid safety track record?
- Do I recognize the importance of support in this new path to explore a deeper level of healing?
- Do I recognize that anxiety about a new experience is an expected natural pause?

- What is my initial response to having a psychedelic experience? Do I believe that I can be supported through my questions and concerns?
- Am I committed to doing the intra and interpersonal work outside of the session to explore areas of change?

7

Using C-KPN Conceptual for Self-Directed Work (REFLECTION GUIDES)

CLIENT REFLECTION:

During the Ketamine Treatment experience, I am overwhelmed and humbled by my capacity to see and experience beyond my normal knowing; I am challenged to find voice and hold on to the knowledge from the experience after the session.

As we conclude our time together, we leave you with journaling guides that you can use before and after each of your Ketamine Treatment sessions to find meaning in the deep nature of the experience. The structure of self reflection will be guided by C-KPN and will bring you back to our foundation: creating potential for yourself when Ego Rigidity is recognized. The work you are doing in your Ketamine Treatment, therapy or wellness pursuits all relate to a deeper connection with your inner strength and having access to the healthiest version of yourself: your Essential and Authentic Self.

The "real" healing begins when you leave the treatment office and return to life with the recognition that something is different. You have the capacity to be active in your exploration and give value to the change potential that may result from treatment. Be patient with yourself and remember this is a journey beginning with where you are. Regardless of where you've been, look forward to this journey. Feelings, emotions, and behavioral tendencies that have been forged from life experiences and may be habitual are not you; they are a part of you that can evolve. The Ketamine experience provides the opportunity to welcome in a more Fluid Ego that is mindful, aware, adaptable, and aspirational.

We hope this book has better prepared you to do your best work in Ketamine Treatment, and more importantly, your best work in life and living. Give yourself permission to explore and find comfort in the fact that more of you is inside and can emerge through Ketamine Treatment. There is hope—**you can change your life.**

KETAMINE SESSION REFLECTION GUIDE

Date of Ketamine Session: _____ Session #: _____

PRE-SESSION REFLECTION:
What I am Feeling/Thinking Prior to Session?

_____

_____

_____

_____

Intentions for Session:
(Examples: Letting go of need to control, surrender, connect to experience, be mindful/aware, aspirational/adaptable)

_____

_____

_____

_____

POST-SESSION REFLECTION:
To begin your post-session reflection, we encourage you to practice 'stream of consciousness' journaling for 5-10 minutes (spontaneously writing down your thoughts, feelings, ideas, and/or reflections as they come to mind, with no particular order or structure).

Predominant Feeling During Experience:
(Examples: conflicted, sad, blissful, connected, etc.)

_____

Self-Assessment of Dissociative Level of Experience (circle):

Low | Moderate | High

Self-Assessment of Experience Feeling (circle):

Reflective/Unwinding | Mindful/Aware | Aspirational/Adaptable

Content of Experience I Would Like to Remember:

1. _____
2. _____
3. _____
4. _____

Recognition of Potential Change:

Current Anxiety Level (circle):

| 1 | 2 | 3 | 4 | 5 | 6 | 7 | 8 | 9 | 10 |

Low   Moderate   High

Current Depression Level (circle):

| 1 | 2 | 3 | 4 | 5 | 6 | 7 | 8 | 9 | 10 |

Low   Moderate   High

Emotional Neutrality in Reflecting on Trauma—*SUDS: Systemic Units of Distress* (Check what aligns with you):

__ Heightened Awareness/Triggering with Emotion
__ Sensing Greater Emotional Neutrality
__ Processing & Access to Inner Healing

Ego Level Self-Assessment (Check what aligns with you):

__ L1: Separated from Life/Living
__ L2: Validating Sense of Threat
__ L3: Need to Control Self/Others
__ L4: Awareness of Damage from My Need to Control Self or Others
__ L5: Openness & Ability to Observe is Replaced by Need for Control (Internal/External)

__ L6: Openness is Restricted by Ego Rigidity—Fear, Shame and Need to Control

__ L7: Open to Seeing the Needs of Others and Choose to Respond

__ L8: Feeling Emotions, Not Being Determined by Them

__ L9: Freedom to Observe, Choose and Respond Freely

Ego Stage Self-Assessment (Check what aligns with you):

__ Stage 1: Survival Mode: Emotional Imbalance

__ Stage 2: Tension Between Openness and Ego Rigidity: The Need to Let Go and Move Forward

__ Stage 3: Ego Flexibility & Resilience: Freedom and Embracing Growth

Connection to Authentic/Essential Self (circle):

Unhealthy/Conflicted | Average/Balanced | Healthy/Aligned

Recognition of Healthy/Unhealthy Coping:

_____

_____

_____

_____

Change Aspiration/Goals: _____

_____

_____

_____

_____

Reflections to Remember for Next Session: _____

_____

_____

_____

_____

Summary Evaluation—Value of Experience in my Life (circle or write your own):

Little/No   Value | Neutral/Unknown | Reflective/Change   Value

_____

_____

_____

_____

_____

_____

_____

_____

_____

_____

_____

_____

_____

_____

_____

_____

_____

_____

_____

KETAMINE SESSION REFLECTION GUIDE

Date of Ketamine Session: _____ Session #: _____

PRE-SESSION REFLECTION:
What I am Feeling/Thinking Prior to Session?

_____

_____

_____

_____

Intentions for Session:
(Examples: Letting go of need to control, surrender, connect to experience, be mindful/aware, aspirational/adaptable)

_____

_____

_____

_____

POST-SESSION REFLECTION:
To begin your post-session reflection, we encourage you to practice 'stream of consciousness' journaling for 5-10 minutes (spontaneously writing down your thoughts, feelings, ideas, and/or reflections as they come to mind, with no particular order or structure).

Predominant Feeling During Experience:
(Examples: conflicted, sad, blissful, connected, etc.)

_____

Self-Assessment of Dissociative Level of Experience (circle):

Low | Moderate | High

Self-Assessment of Experience Feeling (circle):

Reflective/Unwinding | Mindful/Aware | Aspirational/Adaptable

Content of Experience I Would Like to Remember:

1. _____
2. _____
3. _____
4. _____

Recognition of Potential Change:

Current Anxiety Level (circle):

1 | 2 | 3 | 4 | 5 | 6 | 7 | 8 | 9 | 10

Low   Moderate   High

Current Depression Level (circle):

1 | 2 | 3 | 4 | 5 | 6 | 7 | 8 | 9 | 10

Low   Moderate   High

Emotional Neutrality in Reflecting on Trauma—*SUDS: Systemic Units of Distress* (Check what aligns with you):

__ Heightened Awareness/Triggering with Emotion
__ Sensing Greater Emotional Neutrality
__ Processing & Access to Inner Healing

Ego Level Self-Assessment (Check what aligns with you):

__ L1: Separated from Life/Living
__ L2: Validating Sense of Threat
__ L3: Need to Control Self/Others
__ L4: Awareness of Damage from My Need to Control Self or Others
__ L5: Openness & Ability to Observe is Replaced by Need for Control
    (Internal/External)

__ L6: Openness is Restricted by Ego Rigidity—Fear, Shame and Need to Control

__ L7: Open to Seeing the Needs of Others and Choose to Respond

__ L8: Feeling Emotions, Not Being Determined by Them

__ L9: Freedom to Observe, Choose and Respond Freely

Ego Stage Self-Assessment (Check what aligns with you):

__ Stage 1: Survival Mode: Emotional Imbalance

__ Stage 2: Tension Between Openness and Ego Rigidity: The Need to Let Go and Move Forward

__ Stage 3: Ego Flexibility & Resilience: Freedom and Embracing Growth

Connection to Authentic/Essential Self (circle):

Unhealthy/Conflicted | Average/Balanced | Healthy/Aligned

Recognition of Healthy/Unhealthy Coping:

_____

_____

_____

_____

Change Aspiration/Goals: _____

_____

_____

_____

_____

Reflections to Remember for Next Session: _____

_____

_____

_____

_____

Summary Evaluation—Value of Experience in my Life (circle or write your own):

Little/No   Value | Neutral/Unknown | Reflective/Change   Value

_____

_____

_____

_____

_____

_____

_____

_____

_____

_____

_____

_____

_____

_____

_____

_____

_____

_____

_____

_____

KETAMINE SESSION REFLECTION GUIDE

Date of Ketamine Session: _____ Session #: _____

PRE-SESSION REFLECTION:
What I am Feeling/Thinking Prior to Session?

_____

_____

_____

_____

Intentions for Session:
(Examples: Letting go of need to control, surrender, connect to experience, be mindful/aware, aspirational/adaptable)

_____

_____

_____

_____

POST-SESSION REFLECTION:
To begin your post-session reflection, we encourage you to practice 'stream of consciousness' journaling for 5-10 minutes (spontaneously writing down your thoughts, feelings, ideas, and/or reflections as they come to mind, with no particular order or structure).

Predominant Feeling During Experience:
(Examples: conflicted, sad, blissful, connected, etc.)

_____

Self-Assessment of Dissociative Level of Experience (circle):
Low | Moderate | High

Self-Assessment of Experience Feeling (circle):
Reflective/Unwinding | Mindful/Aware | Aspirational/Adaptable

Content of Experience I Would Like to Remember:
1. _____
2. _____
3. _____
4. _____

Recognition of Potential Change:
Current Anxiety Level (circle):

1 | 2 | 3 | 4 | 5 | 6 | 7 | 8 | 9 | 10
Low   Moderate   High

Current Depression Level (circle):

1 | 2 | 3 | 4 | 5 | 6 | 7 | 8 | 9 | 10
Low   Moderate   High

Emotional Neutrality in Reflecting on Trauma—*SUDS: Systemic Units of Distress* (Check what aligns with you):
__ Heightened Awareness/Triggering with Emotion
__ Sensing Greater Emotional Neutrality
__ Processing & Access to Inner Healing

Ego Level Self-Assessment (Check what aligns with you):
__ L1: Separated from Life/Living
__ L2: Validating Sense of Threat
__ L3: Need to Control Self/Others
__ L4: Awareness of Damage from My Need to Control Self or Others
__ L5: Openness & Ability to Observe is Replaced by Need for Control
　　　(Internal/External)

__ L6: Openness is Restricted by Ego Rigidity—Fear, Shame and Need to Control

__ L7: Open to Seeing the Needs of Others and Choose to Respond

__ L8: Feeling Emotions, Not Being Determined by Them

__ L9: Freedom to Observe, Choose and Respond Freely

Ego Stage Self Assessment (Check what aligns with you):

__ Stage 1: Survival Mode: Emotional Imbalance

__ Stage 2: Tension Between Openness and Ego Rigidity: The Need to Let Go and Move Forward

__ Stage 3: Ego Flexibility & Resilience: Freedom and Embracing Growth

Connection to Authentic/Essential Self (circle):

Unhealthy/Conflicted | Average/Balanced | Healthy/Aligned

Recognition of Healthy/Unhealthy Coping:

_____

_____

_____

_____

Change Aspiration/Goals: _____

_____

_____

_____

_____

Reflections to Remember for Next Session: _____

_____

_____

_____

_____

Summary Evaluation—Value of Experience in my Life (circle or write your own):

Little/No   Value | Neutral/Unknown | Reflective/Change   Value

_____

_____

_____

_____

_____

_____

_____

_____

_____

_____

_____

_____

_____

_____

_____

_____

_____

_____

_____

_____

KETAMINE SESSION REFLECTION GUIDE

Date of Ketamine Session: _____ Session #: _____

PRE-SESSION REFLECTION:
What I am Feeling/Thinking Prior to Session?

_____

_____

_____

_____

Intentions for Session:
(Examples: Letting go of need to control, surrender, connect to experience, be mindful/aware, aspirational/adaptable)

_____

_____

_____

_____

POST-SESSION REFLECTION:
To begin your post-session reflection, we encourage you to practice 'stream of consciousness' journaling for 5-10 minutes (spontaneously writing down your thoughts, feelings, ideas, and/or reflections as they come to mind, with no particular order or structure).

Predominant Feeling During Experience:
(Examples: conflicted, sad, blissful, connected, etc.)

_____

Self-Assessment of Dissociative Level of Experience (circle):
Low | Moderate | High

Self-Assessment of Experience Feeling (circle):
Reflective/Unwinding | Mindful/Aware | Aspirational/Adaptable

Content of Experience I Would Like to Remember:
1. _____
2. _____
3. _____
4. _____

Recognition of Potential Change:
Current Anxiety Level (circle):

1 | 2 | 3 | 4 | 5 | 6 | 7 | 8 | 9 | 10
Low   Moderate   High

Current Depression Level (circle):

1 | 2 | 3 | 4 | 5 | 6 | 7 | 8 | 9 | 10
Low   Moderate   High

Emotional Neutrality in Reflecting on Trauma—*SUDS: Systemic Units of Distress* (Check what aligns with you):
__ Heightened Awareness/Triggering with Emotion
__ Sensing Greater Emotional Neutrality
__ Processing & Access to Inner Healing

Ego Level Self-Assessment (Check what aligns with you):
__ L1: Separated from Life/Living
__ L2: Validating Sense of Threat
__ L3: Need to Control Self/Others
__ L4: Awareness of Damage from My Need to Control Self or Others
__ L5: Openness & Ability to Observe is Replaced by Need for Control (Internal/External)

___ L6: Openness is Restricted by Ego Rigidity—Fear, Shame and Need to Control
___ L7: Open to Seeing the Needs of Others and Choose to Respond
___ L8: Feeling Emotions, Not Being Determined by Them
___ L9: Freedom to Observe, Choose and Respond Freely

Ego Stage Self-Assessment (Check what aligns with you):
___ Stage 1: Survival Mode: Emotional Imbalance
___ Stage 2: Tension Between Openness and Ego Rigidity: The Need to Let Go and Move Forward
___ Stage 3: Ego Flexibility & Resilience: Freedom and Embracing Growth

Connection to Authentic/Essential Self (circle):
Unhealthy/Conflicted | Average/Balanced | Healthy/Aligned

Recognition of Healthy/Unhealthy Coping:
_____
_____
_____
_____

Change Aspiration/Goals: _____
_____
_____
_____
_____

Reflections to Remember for Next Session: _____
_____
_____
_____
_____

Summary Evaluation—Value of Experience in my Life (circle or write your own):

Little/No   Value | Neutral/Unknown | Reflective/Change   Value

_____

_____

_____

_____

_____

_____

_____

_____

_____

_____

_____

_____

_____

_____

_____

_____

_____

_____

KETAMINE SESSION REFLECTION GUIDE

Date of Ketamine Session: _____ Session #: _____

PRE-SESSION REFLECTION:
What I am Feeling/Thinking Prior to Session?

_____

_____

_____

_____

Intentions for Session:
(Examples: Letting go of need to control, surrender, connect to experience, be mindful/aware, aspirational/adaptable)

_____

_____

_____

_____

POST-SESSION REFLECTION:
To begin your post-session reflection, we encourage you to practice 'stream of consciousness' journaling for 5-10 minutes (spontaneously writing down your thoughts, feelings, ideas, and/or reflections as they come to mind, with no particular order or structure).

Predominant Feeling During Experience:
(Examples: conflicted, sad, blissful, connected, etc.)

_____

Self Assessment of Dissociative Level of Experience (circle):
Low | Moderate | High

Self Assessment of Experience Feeling (circle):
Reflective/Unwinding | Mindful/Aware | Aspirational/Adaptable

Content of Experience I Would Like to Remember:
1. _____
2. _____
3. _____
4. _____

Recognition of Potential Change:
Current Anxiety Level (circle):

1 | 2 | 3 | 4 | 5 | 6 | 7 | 8 | 9 | 10
Low   Moderate   High

Current Depression Level (circle):

1 | 2 | 3 | 4 | 5 | 6 | 7 | 8 | 9 | 10
Low   Moderate   High

Emotional Neutrality in Reflecting on Trauma—*SUDS: Systemic Units of Distress* (Check what aligns with you):
__ Heightened Awareness/Triggering with Emotion
__ Sensing Greater Emotional Neutrality
__ Processing & Access to Inner Healing

Ego Level Self Assessment (Check what aligns with you):
__ L1: Separated from Life/Living
__ L2: Validating Sense of Threat
__ L3: Need to Control Self/Others
__ L4: Awareness of Damage from My Need to Control Self or Others
__ L5: Openness & Ability to Observe is Replaced by Need for Control (Internal/External)

___ L6: Openness is Restricted by Ego Rigidity—Fear, Shame and Need to Control

___ L7: Open to Seeing the Needs of Others and Choose to Respond

___ L8: Feeling Emotions, Not Being Determined by Them

___ L9: Freedom to Observe, Choose and Respond Freely

Ego Stage Self Assessment (Check what aligns with you):

___ Stage 1: Survival Mode: Emotional Imbalance

___ Stage 2: Tension Between Openness and Ego Rigidity: The Need to Let Go and Move Forward

___ Stage 3: Ego Flexibility & Resilience: Freedom and Embracing Growth

Connection to Authentic/Essential Self (circle):

Unhealthy/Conflicted | Average/Balanced | Healthy/Aligned

Recognition of Healthy/Unhealthy Coping:

_____

_____

_____

_____

Change Aspiration/Goals: _____

_____

_____

_____

Reflections to Remember for Next Session: _____

_____

_____

_____

Summary Evaluation—Value of Experience in my Life (circle or write your own):

Little/No   Value | Neutral/Unknown | Reflective/Change   Value

_____

_____

_____

_____

_____

_____

_____

_____

_____

_____

_____

_____

_____

_____

_____

_____

_____

_____

KETAMINE SESSION REFLECTION GUIDE

Date of Ketamine Session: _____ Session #: _____

PRE-SESSION REFLECTION:
What I am Feeling/Thinking Prior to Session?

_____

_____

_____

_____

Intentions for Session:
(Examples: Letting go of need to control, surrender, connect to experience, be mindful/aware, aspirational/adaptable)

_____

_____

_____

_____

POST-SESSION REFLECTION:
To begin your post-session reflection, we encourage you to practice 'stream of consciousness' journaling for 5-10 minutes (spontaneously writing down your thoughts, feelings, ideas, and/or reflections as they come to mind, with no particular order or structure).

Predominant Feeling During Experience:
(Examples: conflicted, sad, blissful, connected, etc.)

_____

Self-Assessment of Dissociative Level of Experience (circle):

Low | Moderate | High

Self-Assessment of Experience Feeling (circle):

Reflective/Unwinding | Mindful/Aware | Aspirational/Adaptable

Content of Experience I Would Like to Remember:

1. _____
2. _____
3. _____
4. _____

Recognition of Potential Change:

Current Anxiety Level (circle):

1 | 2 | 3 | 4 | 5 | 6 | 7 | 8 | 9 | 10
Low   Moderate   High

Current Depression Level (circle):

1 | 2 | 3 | 4 | 5 | 6 | 7 | 8 | 9 | 10
Low   Moderate   High

Emotional Neutrality in Reflecting on Trauma—*SUDS: Systemic Units of Distress* (Check what aligns with you):

__ Heightened Awareness/Triggering with Emotion

__ Sensing Greater Emotional Neutrality

__ Processing & Access to Inner Healing

Ego Level Self Assessment (Check what aligns with you):

__ L1: Separated from Life/Living

__ L2: Validating Sense of Threat

__ L3: Need to Control Self/Others

__ L4: Awareness of Damage from My Need to Control Self or Others

__ L5: Openness & Ability to Observe is Replaced by Need for Control (Internal/External)

__ L6: Openness is Restricted by Ego Rigidity—Fear, Shame and Need to Control

__ L7: Open to Seeing the Needs of Others and Choose to Respond

__ L8: Feeling Emotions, Not Being Determined by Them

__ L9: Freedom to Observe, Choose and Respond Freely

Ego Stage Self-Assessment (Check what aligns with you):

__ Stage 1: Survival Mode: Emotional Imbalance

__ Stage 2: Tension Between Openness and Ego Rigidity: The Need to Let Go and Move Forward

__ Stage 3: Ego Flexibility & Resilience: Freedom and Embracing Growth

Connection to Authentic/Essential Self (circle):

Unhealthy/Conflicted | Average/Balanced | Healthy/Aligned

Recognition of Healthy/Unhealthy Coping:

_____

_____

_____

_____

Change Aspiration/Goals: _____

_____

_____

_____

_____

Reflections to Remember for Next Session: _____

_____

_____

_____

_____

Summary Evaluation—Value of Experience in my Life (circle or write your own):

Little/No Value | Neutral/Unknown | Reflective/Change Value

_____

_____

_____

_____

_____

_____

_____

_____

_____

_____

_____

_____

_____

_____

_____

_____

_____

_____

_____

KETAMINE SESSION REFLECTION GUIDE

Date of Ketamine Session: _____ Session #: _____

PRE-SESSION REFLECTION:
What I am Feeling/Thinking Prior to Session?

_____

_____

_____

_____

Intentions for Session:
(Examples: Letting go of need to control, surrender, connect to experience, be mindful/aware, aspirational/adaptable)

_____

_____

_____

_____

POST-SESSION REFLECTION:
To begin your post-session reflection, we encourage you to practice 'stream of consciousness' journaling for 5-10 minutes (spontaneously writing down your thoughts, feelings, ideas, and/or reflections as they come to mind, with no particular order or structure).

Predominant Feeling During Experience:
(Examples: conflicted, sad, blissful, connected, etc.)

_____

Self-Assessment of Dissociative Level of Experience (circle):

Low | Moderate | High

Self-Assessment of Experience Feeling (circle):

Reflective/Unwinding | Mindful/Aware | Aspirational/Adaptable

Content of Experience I Would Like to Remember:

1. _____

2. _____

3. _____

4. _____

Recognition of Potential Change:

Current Anxiety Level (circle):

1 | 2 | 3 | 4 | 5 | 6 | 7 | 8 | 9 | 10
Low   Moderate   High

Current Depression Level (circle):

1 | 2 | 3 | 4 | 5 | 6 | 7 | 8 | 9 | 10
Low   Moderate   High

Emotional Neutrality in Reflecting on Trauma—*SUDS: Systemic Units of Distress* (Check what aligns with you):

__ Heightened Awareness/Triggering with Emotion

__ Sensing Greater Emotional Neutrality

__ Processing & Access to Inner Healing

Ego Level Self Assessment (Check what aligns with you):

__ L1: Separated from Life/Living

__ L2: Validating Sense of Threat

__ L3: Need to Control Self/Others

__ L4: Awareness of Damage from My Need to Control Self or Others

__ L5: Openness & Ability to Observe is Replaced by Need for Control (Internal/External)

__ L6: Openness is Restricted by Ego Rigidity—Fear, Shame and Need to Control
__ L7: Open to Seeing the Needs of Others and Choose to Respond
__ L8: Feeling Emotions, Not Being Determined by Them
__ L9: Freedom to Observe, Choose and Respond Freely

Ego Stage Self-Assessment (Check what aligns with you):
__ Stage 1: Survival Mode: Emotional Imbalance
__ Stage 2: Tension Between Openness and Ego Rigidity: The Need to Let Go and Move Forward
__ Stage 3: Ego Flexibility & Resilience: Freedom and Embracing Growth

Connection to Authentic/Essential Self (circle):

Unhealthy/Conflicted | Average/Balanced | Healthy/Aligned

Recognition of Healthy/Unhealthy Coping:

_____
_____
_____
_____

Change Aspiration/Goals: _____

_____
_____
_____
_____

Reflections to Remember for Next Session: _____

_____
_____
_____
_____

Summary Evaluation—Value of Experience in my Life (circle or write your own):

Little/No Value | Neutral/Unknown | Reflective/Change Value

_____

_____

_____

_____

_____

_____

_____

_____

_____

_____

_____

_____

_____

_____

_____

_____

_____

_____

KETAMINE SESSION REFLECTION GUIDE

Date of Ketamine Session: _____ Session #: _____

PRE-SESSION REFLECTION:
What I am Feeling/Thinking Prior to Session?

_____

_____

_____

_____

Intentions for Session:
(Examples: Letting go of need to control, surrender, connect to experience, be mindful/aware, aspirational/adaptable)

_____

_____

_____

_____

POST-SESSION REFLECTION:
To begin your post-session reflection, we encourage you to practice 'stream of consciousness' journaling for 5-10 minutes (spontaneously writing down your thoughts, feelings, ideas, and/or reflections as they come to mind, with no particular order or structure).

Predominant Feeling During Experience:
(Examples: conflicted, sad, blissful, connected, etc.)

_____

Self-Assessment of Dissociative Level of Experience (circle):
Low | Moderate | High

Self-Assessment of Experience Feeling (circle):
Reflective/Unwinding | Mindful/Aware | Aspirational/Adaptable

Content of Experience I Would Like to Remember:
1. _____
2. _____
3. _____
4. _____

Recognition of Potential Change:
Current Anxiety Level (circle):

1 | 2 | 3 | 4 | 5 | 6 | 7 | 8 | 9 | 10

Low   Moderate   High

Current Depression Level (circle):

1 | 2 | 3 | 4 | 5 | 6 | 7 | 8 | 9 | 10

Low   Moderate   High

Emotional Neutrality in Reflecting on Trauma—*SUDS: Systemic Units of Distress* (Check what aligns with you):
__ Heightened Awareness/Triggering with Emotion
__ Sensing Greater Emotional Neutrality
__ Processing & Access to Inner Healing

Ego Level Self Assessment (Check what aligns with you):
__ L1: Separated from Life/Living
__ L2: Validating Sense of Threat
__ L3: Need to Control Self/Others
__ L4: Awareness of Damage from My Need to Control Self or Others
__ L5: Openness & Ability to Observe is Replaced by Need for Control (Internal/External)

__ L6: Openness is Restricted by Ego Rigidity—Fear, Shame and Need to Control

__ L7: Open to Seeing the Needs of Others and Choose to Respond

__ L8: Feeling Emotions, Not Being Determined by Them

__ L9: Freedom to Observe, Choose and Respond Freely

Ego Stage Self-Assessment (Check what aligns with you):

__ Stage 1: Survival Mode: Emotional Imbalance

__ Stage 2: Tension Between Openness and Ego Rigidity: The Need to Let Go and Move Forward

__ Stage 3: Ego Flexibility & Resilience: Freedom and Embracing Growth

Connection to Authentic/Essential Self (circle):

Unhealthy/Conflicted | Average/Balanced | Healthy/Aligned

Recognition of Healthy/Unhealthy Coping:

_____

_____

_____

_____

Change Aspiration/Goals: _____

_____

_____

_____

_____

Reflections to Remember for Next Session: _____

_____

_____

_____

_____

Summary Evaluation—Value of Experience in my Life (circle or write your own):

Little/No Value | Neutral/Unknown | Reflective/Change Value

_____

_____

_____

_____

_____

_____

_____

_____

_____

_____

_____

_____

_____

_____

_____

_____

_____

KETAMINE SESSION REFLECTION GUIDE

Date of Ketamine Session: _____ Session #: _____

PRE-SESSION REFLECTION:
What I am Feeling/Thinking Prior to Session?

_____

_____

_____

_____

Intentions for Session:
(Examples: Letting go of need to control, surrender, connect to experience, be mindful/aware, aspirational/adaptable)

_____

_____

_____

_____

POST-SESSION REFLECTION:
To begin your post-session reflection, we encourage you to practice 'stream of consciousness' journaling for 5-10 minutes (spontaneously writing down your thoughts, feelings, ideas, and/or reflections as they come to mind, with no particular order or structure).

Predominant Feeling During Experience:
(Examples: conflicted, sad, blissful, connected, etc.)

_____

Self-Assessment of Dissociative Level of Experience (circle):
Low | Moderate | High

Self-Assessment of Experience Feeling (circle):
Reflective/Unwinding | Mindful/Aware | Aspirational/Adaptable

Content of Experience I Would Like to Remember:
1. _____
2. _____
3. _____
4. _____

Recognition of Potential Change:
Current Anxiety Level (circle):

1 | 2 | 3 | 4 | 5 | 6 | 7 | 8 | 9 | 10
Low   Moderate   High

Current Depression Level (circle):

1 | 2 | 3 | 4 | 5 | 6 | 7 | 8 | 9 | 10
Low   Moderate   High

Emotional Neutrality in Reflecting on Trauma—*SUDS: Systemic Units of Distress* (Check what aligns with you):
__ Heightened Awareness/Triggering with Emotion
__ Sensing Greater Emotional Neutrality
__ Processing & Access to Inner Healing

Ego Level Self Assessment (Check what aligns with you):
__ L1: Separated from Life/Living
__ L2: Validating Sense of Threat
__ L3: Need to Control Self/Others
__ L4: Awareness of Damage from My Need to Control Self or Others
__ L5: Openness & Ability to Observe is Replaced by Need for Control (Internal/External)

__ L6: Openness is Restricted by Ego Rigidity—Fear, Shame and Need to Control

__ L7: Open to Seeing the Needs of Others and Choose to Respond

__ L8: Feeling Emotions, Not Being Determined by Them

__ L9: Freedom to Observe, Choose and Respond Freely

Ego Stage Self-Assessment (Check what aligns with you):

__ Stage 1: Survival Mode: Emotional Imbalance

__ Stage 2: Tension Between Openness and Ego Rigidity: The Need to Let Go and Move Forward

__ Stage 3: Ego Flexibility & Resilience: Freedom and Embracing Growth

Connection to Authentic/Essential Self (circle):

Unhealthy/Conflicted | Average/Balanced | Healthy/Aligned

Recognition of Healthy/Unhealthy Coping:

_____

_____

_____

_____

Change Aspiration/Goals: _____

_____

_____

_____

_____

Reflections to Remember for Next Session: _____

_____

_____

_____

_____

Summary Evaluation—Value of Experience in my Life (circle or write your own):

Little/No Value | Neutral/Unknown | Reflective/Change Value

_____

_____

_____

_____

_____

_____

_____

_____

_____

_____

_____

_____

_____

_____

_____

_____

_____

_____

_____

_____

KETAMINE SESSION REFLECTION GUIDE

Date of Ketamine Session: _____ Session #: _____

PRE-SESSION REFLECTION:

What I am Feeling/Thinking Prior to Session?

_____
_____
_____
_____

Intentions for Session:

(Examples: Letting go of need to control, surrender, connect to experience, be mindful/aware, aspirational/adaptable)

_____
_____
_____
_____

POST-SESSION REFLECTION:

To begin your post-session reflection, we encourage you to practice 'stream of consciousness' journaling for 5-10 minutes (spontaneously writing down your thoughts, feelings, ideas, and/or reflections as they come to mind, with no particular order or structure).

Predominant Feeling During Experience:

(Examples: conflicted, sad, blissful, connected, etc.)

Self-Assessment of Dissociative Level of Experience (circle):
Low | Moderate | High

Self-Assessment of Experience Feeling (circle):
Reflective/Unwinding | Mindful/Aware | Aspirational/Adaptable

Content of Experience I Would Like to Remember:
1. _____
2. _____
3. _____
4. _____

Recognition of Potential Change:
Current Anxiety Level (circle):

1 | 2 | 3 | 4 | 5 | 6 | 7 | 8 | 9 | 10

Low   Moderate   High

Current Depression Level (circle):

1 | 2 | 3 | 4 | 5 | 6 | 7 | 8 | 9 | 10

Low   Moderate   High

Emotional Neutrality in Reflecting on Trauma—*SUDS: Systemic Units of Distress* (Check what aligns with you):
__ Heightened Awareness/Triggering with Emotion
__ Sensing Greater Emotional Neutrality
__ Processing & Access to Inner Healing

Ego Level Self Assessment (Check what aligns with you):
__ L1: Separated from Life/Living
__ L2: Validating Sense of Threat
__ L3: Need to Control Self/Others
__ L4: Awareness of Damage from My Need to Control Self or Others
__ L5: Openness & Ability to Observe is Replaced by Need for Control
       (Internal/External)

__ L6: Openness is Restricted by Ego Rigidity—Fear, Shame and Need to Control

__ L7: Open to Seeing the Needs of Others and Choose to Respond

__ L8: Feeling Emotions, Not Being Determined by Them

__ L9: Freedom to Observe, Choose and Respond Freely

Ego Stage Self-Assessment (Check what aligns with you):

__ Stage 1: Survival Mode: Emotional Imbalance

__ Stage 2: Tension Between Openness and Ego Rigidity: The Need to Let Go and Move Forward

__ Stage 3: Ego Flexibility & Resilience: Freedom and Embracing Growth

Connection to Authentic/Essential Self (circle):

Unhealthy/Conflicted | Average/Balanced | Healthy/Aligned

Recognition of Healthy/Unhealthy Coping:

_____

_____

_____

_____

Change Aspiration/Goals: _____

_____

_____

_____

Reflections to Remember for Next Session: _____

_____

_____

_____

Summary Evaluation—Value of Experience in my Life (circle or write your own):

Little/No   Value | Neutral/Unknown | Reflective/Change   Value

_____

_____

_____

_____

_____

_____

_____

_____

_____

_____

_____

_____

_____

_____

_____

_____

_____

_____

ACKNOWLEDGMENTS

We would be remiss not to recognize the hard work of many who supported the development of this book. Thank you for your contributions:

Dr. Tee Todd (MD)
Providing writing assistance in Chapter 5 and providing medical support to clients being served at Attento Counseling.

Vanessa Crenshaw (LPC, Director–Attento Counseling)
Your investment in guiding the process of book development and keeping us focused on the needs of potential clients has been invaluable.

Raina Williams (Administrative Manager–Attento Counseling)
From logistics to maintaining our team's focus–your leadership has guided us through this process.

Lily Neuhaus (Professional Editor/Writer)
The editing force that kept us on message in finding the voice to speak to the target audience we so passionately wish to support.

Dr. Naveen Thomas (MD, Clarity Integrative Psychiatry)
Our subject matter expert on all things Ketamine and partner in developing our Practice.

Our Ketamine LPC Service Team (Danielle Greene, Jennifer Caruso, Jeff Brannan, Beth Ebinger)
Your valued input and hours of work with clients has made this book possible.

DR. LES COLE has over 45 years of experience as a passionate practitioner in the field of mental health, spirituality, and psychology. He has historically divided his time between development, clinical practice, training, clinical supervision, and consulting. He regularly provides workshops and seminars for Foster Parents, parenting, team building, the Enneagram, and trauma. Dr. Cole has had the privilege of witnessing dramatic transformations working with clients with depression, anxiety disorders, suicidal ideation, personality disorders, chronic illness, and trauma disorders. He is eager to apply his experience and compassion with clients, families, couples, and teens as they begin to address issues that will help them to improve their quality of life and attain a sense of fulfillment. Dr. Cole is licensed as a professional counselor by the State of Georgia, a Certified Professional Counselor Supervisor and Certified Clinical Trauma Professional.

Enjoying a 35 plus year career in both public and private human services, **DR. TIM GIANNONI** has remained dedicated to a single priority of exploring how direct service intervention can enhance personal potential. From a humble awakening as a counselor for economically disadvantaged youth to managing large nonprofit and public organizations, he has remained committed to the application of research and ideas into practice. Dr. Giannoni has come to appreciate that psychological variables are an integral part of life and living interaction. His passion has remained steadfast to support others in seeing beyond the limits of presenting "normal" in the pursuit of actively exploring and embracing change—a challenge he has also faced. Dr. Giannoni's focus is the belief that ongoing work over the years has contributed to improvement in the human condition. Through many years of education, direct service and leadership opportunities to be of service to others, his goal has been to respond with compassion and while continuing his own work of self-growth and development. Dr. Giannoni's direct work with Ketamine intervention over these past four years has enabled him to see and truly believe mind-level change is possible and can be achieved more expeditiously with proper treatment and support. He feels he has been given the gift of a unique experience that offers promise for many. Lastly, Dr. Giannoni would like to give a resounding thank you to his life-long partner and wife Gigi who has always provided unconditional support in exploring change to find the best version of himself.

REFERENCES

CHAPTER 1

1. Saint-Laurent, R., & Bird, S. (2015, March 26). Somatic experiencing: How trauma can be overcome. *Psychology Today*. https://www.psychologytoday.com/us/blog/the-intelligent-divorce/201503/somatic-experiencing.

2. Zimberoff, D., & Hartman, D. (2000). The ego in heart-centered therapies: Ego strengthening and ego surrender. *Journal of Heart Centered Therapies*, 3(2), 3. https://link.gale.com/apps/doc/A7422152/AONE?u =anon-75acd844&sid=googleScholar&xid=4f585eb5

3. Davey, C. G., Pujol, J., & Harrison, B. J. (2016). Mapping the self in the brain's default mode network. *Neuroimage*, 132, 390-397. http://dx.doi.org/10.1016/j.neuroimage.2016.02.022.

4. Zimberoff, D., & Hartman, M. A. D. (1999). Personal transformation with heart-centered therapies. *Journal of Heart Centered Therapies*, 2, 3-53.

5. Öhman, A. (2005). The role of the amygdala in human fear: Automatic detection of threat. *Psychoneuroendocrinology*, 30(10), 953-958. https://doi.org/10.1016/ j.psyneuen.2005.03.019.

6. Öhman, A. (2005). The role of the amygdala in human fear: Automatic detection of threat. *Psychoneuroendocrinology*, 30(10), 953-958. https://doi.org/10.1016/ j.psyneuen.2005.03.019.

7. Kolk, B. A. (2003). The neurobiology of childhood trauma and abuse. *Child and Adolescent Psychiatric Clinics of North America*, 12(2), 293-317. https://doi.org/10.1016/S1056-4993(03) 00003-8.

8. Saint-Laurent, R., & Bird, S. (2015, March 26). Somatic experiencing: How trauma can be overcome. *Psychology Today*. https://www.psychologytoday.com/us/blog/the- intelligent-divorce/201503/somatic-experiencing.

9. Winnicott, D. W. (1986). The theory of the parent-infant relationship. *Essential papers on object relations*, 233-253.

10. Maree, J. G. (2021). The psychosocial development theory of Erik Erikson: Critical overview. *Early Child Development and Care*, 191(7-8), 1107-1121. https://doi.org/ 10.1080/03004430.2020.1845163.

11. Moran, J. M., Kelley, W. M., & Heatherton, T. F. (2013). What can the organization of the brain's default mode network tell us about self-knowledge? *Frontiers in Human Neuroscience*, 7(391), 1-6. https://doi.org/10.3389/fnhum.2013.00391.

12. Mars, R. B., Neubert, F., Noonan, M. P., Sallet, J., Toni, I., & Rushworth, M. F. S. (2012). On the relationship between the "default mode network" and the "social brain". *Frontiers in Human Neuroscience*, 6(189), 1-9. https://doi.org/10.3389/fnhum.2012.00189.

13. Winnicott, D. W. (1986). The theory of the parent-infant relationship. *Essential papers on object relations*, 233-253.

14. Orders of change. (2022, December 27). *Integral Eye Movement Therapy; The Association for IEMT Practitioners*. https://integraleyemovementtherapy.wiki/orders_of_change.

CHAPTER 2

1. Demarin, V., & Morovic, S. (2014). Neuroplasticity. *Periodicum Biologorum*, 116(2), 209-211.

2 Rafferty, A. E., Jimmieson, N. L., & Armenakis, A. A. (2013). Change readiness: A multilevel review. *Journal of Management*, 39(1), 110-135. https://doi.org/10.1177/ 0149206312457417.

CHAPTER 3

1. Nelson, P. (2018). *There's a hole in my sidewalk: The romance of self-discovery*. Atria Paperbacks.

2. *Suffering is optional*. Wilcox & Barton. (2018, September 5). https://www.wilcoxandbarton.com/news-resources/Suffering-Is-Optional-entry-34.

3. Riso, D. R. & Hudson, R. (1996). *Personality types: Using the enneagram for self-discovery*. Houghton Mifflin Company.

4. Riso, D. R. & Hudson, R. (1999). *The wisdom of the enneagram: The complete guide to psychological and spiritual growth for the nine personality types*. Bantam Books.

5. Miller, R., & Dillman Taylor, D. (2016). Does Adlerian theory stand the test of time?: Examining individual psychology from a neuroscience perspective. *The Journal of Humanistic Counseling*, 55(2), 111-128.

CHAPTER 5

1. Gill, H., Gill, B., Rodrigues, N. B., Lipsitz, O., Rosenblat, J. D., El-Halabi, S., Nasri, F., Mansur, R. B., Lee, Y., & McIntyre, R. S. (2021) The effects of ketamine on cognition in treatment-resistant depression: A systematic review and priority avenues for future research. *Neuroscience & Biobehavioral Reviews*, 120, 78-85. https://doi.org/10.1016/j.neubiorev.2020.11.020.

2. Kohtala, S. (2021). Ketamine—50 years in use: From anesthesia to rapid antidepressant effects and neurobiological mechanisms. *Pharmacological Reports*, 73(2), 323-345.

3. Zarate, C. A. (2020). Ketamine: A new chapter in antidepressant development. *Brazilian Journal of Psychiatry*, 42(6), 581-582. https://doi.org/10.1590/1516-4446-2020-1000.

4. Voineskos, D., Daskalakis, Z. J., & Blumberger, D. M. (2020). Management of treatment-resistant depression: Challenges and strategies. *Neuropsychiatr Dis Treat*, 16, 221-234. https://doi.org/10.2147/NDT.S198774

5. Zhang, Y., Ye, F., Zhang, T., Lv, S., Zhou, L., Du, D., ... & Zhu, S. (2021). Structural basis of Ketamine action on human NMDA receptors. *Nature*, 596(7871), 301-305.

6. Zanos, P., & Gould, T. (2018). Mechanisms of ketamine action as an antidepressant. *Molecular Psychiatry*, 23(4), 801-811.

7. Szarmach, J., Cubała, W. J., Włodarczyk, A., & Gałuszko-Węgielnik, M. (2020). Metabolic risk factors and cardiovascular safety in Ketamine use for treatment resistant depression. *Neuropsychiatric Disease and Treatment*, 16, 25-39.

8. Rosenbaum, S. B., Gupta, V., Patel, P., & Palacios, J. L. (2022, November 24). *Ketamine*. National Library of Medicine. https://www.ncbi.nlm.nih.gov/books/NBK470357/

9. Woolfe, S. (2022, November 1). *Is Ketamine Addictive? Experts Weigh In*. HealingMaps. https://healingmaps.com/is-ketamine-addictive/.

CHAPTER 6

1.Ezquerra-Romano, I. I., Lawn, W., Krupitsky, E., & Morgan, C. J. A. (2018). Ketamine for the treatment of addiction: Evidence and potential mechanisms. *Neuropharmacology*, 142, 72-82. https://doi.org/10.1016/j.neuropharm.2018.01.017.

2. Riso, D. R. & Hudson, R. (1999). The Triadic Self. In *The wisdom of the enneagram: The complete guide to psychological and spiritual growth for the nine personality types*. (pp. 49-68). Bantam Books.

Made in United States
Troutdale, OR
04/15/2024

19209013R00086